UHURU KENYATTA CASE:
THE ICC FACTOR.

TRACING THE ROOT OF
THE CONSPIRACY.

BY

JOSEPH   NDUNGU.

SPIRITUAL SIGNIFICANT OF MUNGIKI AND

'ISLAMIC CALIPHATE'.

WITNESS ACCOUNT.

They were all trapped, politicians, church leaders, tribes, young and old by a "jinn", a devil in a person, who came saying "Thaai", peace but it turned to be a lie. Could this be a sign, to the end time?

1st. Thessalonians 5:3. Take heed, that those days should not overtake you.

Dedicated to those that seek truth, for truth is God. And truth sets free.

Email:wndungu2@gmail.com.

The eagle is the only bird that soar above any other bird, it's vision is super, it is a patient bird, no other bird can go beyond the soaring of an eagle and God liken himself as an eagle. Our calling in these age is symbolized and characterized as an eagle to see from an eye of super optical angle and soar above the forces of evil with truth, confidence and strength.
Break up from the ties of your, race, color, tribe, clan nation and religion, your closed heart and preconceived judgment only enslaves your potential and gravity will always pull you down but eagles overcomes the force of gravity soaring high above powerful winds and with a clear vision they can see and understand, the present, the past and what the future holds.

Special thanks To.

David W Wagacha

For his contributions.

The International criminal court for standing in the gap and pointing a finger.

To the victims, you were not alone, we were all trapped, By an evil seed.

Events are permitted by God for a lesson.

CONTENTS.

INTRODUCTION.

The ultimate purpose of life is to realize love in its full strength, character should be what that defines humans. The way of true knowledge, love goes beyond measure and it cuts through boundaries that humans associate themselves with, love doesn't profile humans into tribes, race, clans, color religion and geographical areas judging them through these factors, though we are humanly positioned by birth, clan, tribe, nation, race, color or religion and in certain geographical areas for a purpose.

Our mission here on earth is to identify our obligation and serves the purpose of God in the way of love and that's by its knowledge. Our mental maturity should define our being, lessons we may have learned, witnessed, heard or observed as events unfold. That should be what that defines people, their individual character. That alone should be the only primary element that defines who we are and with that, our souls move to a different dimension that identifies with our master creator.

I write these book with a tag of a Kikuyu name but love has cut through the ties with my human origin though born in Rift valley, a province in The Republic of Kenya, a Nation in Africa. By lineal descent, I'm from a clan called "ethaga" of the Kikuyu tribe and by race a black African born again Christian, a disciple of our Lord Jesus Christ.

I call myself a disciple of our Lord Jesus Christ because it is the Lord himself who have truly taught me through prophetic unfolding events and as in the Bible days and as one who have witnessed, heard and seen these things, the events that unfolds my writing, I'm obligated to humanity, to Kenya, to Christians, to God and my fellow tribesmen where I deprive my name Waithaka, a name they would have wished I should not have possessed, I'm seen as a traitor to the community deep guarded secrets, dark secrets that every community hold, a hidden past that many shy to speak about but for their good I was born among them.

I write down what I saw, witnessed, heard or observed as actual truthful events and by grace of God, may these help any predestined seed of God to learn, understand the mystery that surrounds mental slavery that we humans have unconsciously been imprisoned into.

Though boastfully we pride ourselves among the knowledgeable, spiritual and godly we are blind, naked, poor and miserable and our ego won't let us humbly submit to truth because by way of our birth, our clan, tribe, nation race, color or religion, ego has elevated our souls and spirits to believing we are a special superior breed of people and by so doing we remain in an oblivion of mental slavery that places our being into hell, present hell waiting for the real hell to unfold.

By all standards all humans are guilty for in all their doings, their inner conscious of profiling others condemns them, Nations have felt superior to others, tribes, clans and races alike, but true knowledge condemns all and though the way of love opens its gates wide, faith being our first steps, humans fail to grasp grace that would enable them live harmoniously and peacefully with each other.

I'm not a writer, so please bear with my simple English, style or whatever you may find intellectually wrong, for the purpose of the writing is not to parade myself as a writer, a storyteller or an entertainer but to account events as a witness, a truthful witness, a duty I'm bound by a moral obligation to pass to you as a testimony of the nature of the hypocritical world we live today.

The human race is and has always been in a mental bondage , enslavement of a worse kind than physical slavery, likened to hell to be exact but my case study rests on what our Lord Jesus Christ have enabled me to witness, what I saw and observed unfold, I'm therefore not giving you an interpretation of my thinking but a witness account, though at the end of this I will give my own personal observation on a particular events and also some comparison of a what I saw, heard or observed, I tried to partner with elites, the powerful political personalities but God won't let me, I'm a former witness of The case of The Prosecutor Vs Uhuru Kenyatta, The President of Republic of Kenya at The International Criminal Court of the Hague Netherlands.

The prosecutor Vs Uhuru Kenyatta.

Spiritual science is a study of behavioral nature of spirits and with research and longtime of observation one can learn a pattern that relates to different kinds of demonic spirits manifestation having their source as one deity called, Satan, Lucifer, the evil one, devil and etc.

Through mutation and transformation, they try to establish some sort of jurisdiction of control, through certain believes as a tribe, religion, race clan and etc. and the prince demons establish caliphates', Kingdoms, whose power and authority is absolute. Spiritual Kingdoms that according to their messengers, their missions are prophetic, they copy and transform themselves as angels of light.

Through lineal descent, I happened to be born a Kikuyu, "a mwithaga" by clan and my cousins, sons of my paternal uncle were Mungiki leaders, Mungiki is a dreaded tribal militias group that has its roots in the founding fathers of the Kenya Republic, the freedom fighters -the Mau Mau.

Charles Ndungu Wagacha a 'former Mungiki acting chairman' executed in cold blood by government militias code named Kwekwe squad, George Njoroge Wagacha, killed along with Maina Njenga wife, [Maina Njenga is the spiritual leader of Mungiki] Mungiki Mysterious religion, David Waithaka Wagacha, and Joe Waiganjo Ngigi, 'a former Mungiki spokesman, all are my paternal cousins, sons of my uncles. Maina Njenga happens also to be a distant cousin.

I was also brought up in Eldoret, my neighbors' from this village were the victims of the kiambaa Church burning where women, children and other villagers were burnt alive in the name of tribal identity baptized political indifference.

I'm a beneficially of hard working parents who tirelessly worked hard and acquired a small piece of land in the outskirts of Eldoret, I had started school in St Columbans Turbo and later went to Flax Boarding Kaptagat, I was born a third born son. My older sister and brother had passed on earlier before I was 20, therefore becoming a first born son of my mother with some responsibility ahead.

After secondary school education, I joined Griffins' college Nairobi for sales and marketing training, I faced the world like any other young adult eager to explore what life had to offer.

My last job before the devil came rolling was with Beta-Healthcare Int,' formerly Boots company Plc. In the year 2000, I resigned from this job after I felt disturbed on the trend of repetitive tribal clashes, which I had witnessed in 1992 and 1997 while working in Nakuru and Mombasa respectively.

In 1992, we were victims of these clashes and we lost our farm my father had sweated over the years to develop, and though the farm was just a few acres of land, it was adequate and we never lacked food and other basic human necessities. My father had died at a young age of 45, a year after my sister's death when I was just 21 years. My mother being a hard working lady, a mum who knew nothing else besides farm work, she had worked hard to raise my other siblings, but sometimes life has some events that unless explained from a spiritual perceptive, human efforts and dreams are shattered in a single moment. God had blessed her efforts and was very supportive, she did all she could as a single parent to educate all my siblings.

My mother moved from Eldoret and settled in Kiambu in a small 50x 100 ft. plot that became her new" farm "and hard times were ahead for us, though by God's grace I had a good job as a van salesman with Beta healthcare Int, and she wasn't alone I was beside her but the trauma and my experience of what I had witnessed earlier of helpless village mothers fleeing their homes in the 1992 tribal clashes haunted me.

In the year 2000, I thought the problem of tribal clashes ought to be openly dealt with and addressed in a transparent and truthful manner because we knew some government officials were involved, Powerful personalities in the 'former President Daniel Moi government were mentioned in the tribal clashes reports by Kiliku commission and Akiwumi commission pointing fingers to several of former President Moi colonies.' I felt concerned and made a decision to confront this problem. My innocence nearly costed my life I had not known politics were that evil until when I was in the circles of those that decided and made Kenya look politically ugly.

My instincts and live conscious of choice of evil and good made enemies and disagreed with many and when I couldn't bear, I thought I might had made a wrong choice to question the integrity of these politicians but it was too late, I was already marked as an enemy.

My cousins had by now established themselves as Mungiki leaders, a movement by then I had thought that was just a religious organization that believed in Kikuyu traditional teaching, they had grown to be a force that had influence in politics and were already dining with high profile politicians. In the years 1991-2000, Mungiki to an outsider portrayed an image of innocent disciplined young youths.

I thought with their disciplined members whom I had admired for openly speaking about the evil in our society, were a force that needed political direction that would see them in parliament and address tribal clashes, corruption and bad governance, I saw a ready support of volunteers who could be trusted as genuine citizens who wanted nothing beside truth. I was in for a shock to realize the other 'side of the coin'.

I called my cousin Joe Waiganjo who later took me to see Maina Njenga, I introduced my ideas to them of getting youth support to wrestle the existing Kikuyu leaders whom we had all agreed that were corrupt and were not addressing the problems facing the community, I didn't know I had crossed the border and I was no longer in Kenya I knew, but a foreign different Kingdom, an ethnic-caliphate called" Kirinyaga Kingdom".

 I was lured by Maina Njenga to a meeting in Thika town after few days of interaction with the Mungiki, to address the youth on the next course of action in politics. We arrived and after a brief introduction, I was led to a location where a feast was going on. I was immediately directed to door where I was ushered to pick a piece of meat, hell started beckoning, I was shown a door and as soon as I entered a second room, a dark room with no windows, whips with young men rained on me, with words in kikuyu"uyu ni thingira wa gikuyu",this is the house of Mumbi [Mumbi is believed to be the Eve the of Gikuyu tribe as the Adam and Eve in the Bible],"remove your clothes", "remove your clothes", others telling me "here we speak in whisper", having seen another naked person in that room and whips raining on me, I was confused and before I could compose myself to understand what was happening, I just found myself asking them to spare the me I'm complying. With whisper from a corner, I could hear words, "this is Kikuyu altar and even Kimathi passed here", the kikuyu legend Mau Mau warrior," remove your clothes" or "you suffer the consequences", My fear propelled me to obey and in the next few minutes, I was facing an altar of assorted paraphernalia and repeating some words as I was commanded by an oath administrator. Facing the oath administrator and naked, I was swearing, "If I reveal this secret may this oath kill me, if I reveal this oath, may this goat kill me".

 Though I really felt bad about the oath, I never followed their instruction or attended a "batoni", Platoon meeting as was required and by having my cousins as leaders, I thought I was excused, or they thought, I belonged to their platoon that was called "J5",This conspiracy of recruiting Kikuyu army Militias to defend the community and to be handy in times when called for was the core factor that Kikuyu leaders admired from Mungiki and Mungiki was a "jewel" when tribal clashes started in Rift valley and a cry of help echoed in Central Province. Who planted this seed? Let's go together,

 The Mungiki leadership and the Kikuyu tribal leaders made a secret conspiracy that was the basis of the investigation that landed Uhuru Kenyatta the president of the Republic of Kenya to The Hague, Netherlands with the charges, of crimes against humanity, murder, rape, deportation, displacement of population and other inhuman acts.

A clean up on what had transpired during these clashes had to be done by the then Kibaki administration, Hon. John Michuki,' former internal security Minister' got a shock and died after learning what he had thought would never be known was now in an open court and he couldn't face or comprehend the outcome.

His life couldn't hold to that reality he died, Hon George Saitoti, also a 'former internal security minister', Hon George Thuo 'former Juja M.P' and a batch of Mungiki leaders had to shut up and their mouths had to remain shut.

 By fate or destiny, God positioned me as a truthful witness, most credible, honest, nonpartisan and truthfully trustworthy to give a factual account and with my conscious only answerable to God, I'm morally obligated to write a truthful account of events as I know them having being in the midst of all these, my former neighbors' being victims of this tribal animosity, my cousins being leaders of the Kikuyu militias with a backing of powerful Kikuyu tribe personalities.

I'm willing to shed some light and unlock the mystery that surrounds Mungiki, trace the seed of tribal clashes as from 1992, shed some light in the case The Prosecutor Vs Uhuru Kenyatta and give a lead from any perspective that can be relied on as a research manual for a scholar, or a historian willing to straighten up records that surrounds these events. It's also a guide to preachers there, who imprisons many in the name of God serving tribal partisan interests, denying faith and positioning themselves as 'tribal Christians elders', titles unknown in the Bible. These respected Christian leaders hypocritically engaged in these acts of conspiracy in the name of political expediency and in their blindness, they lead many astray.

This should be a lesson and a soul searching reflection, to all these leaders for to their shame, they have enslaved and continue to enslave many in a hell bondage, spiritual slavery, a physical hell on earth waiting for an everlasting one to unfold.

The international Criminal court can also use this as a guide, a lead, a manual for them to understand that though by name they exist, they lack the teeth to bite and they are powerless, their muscle can only be exercised through decisions by United Nations security council, they lack honest motivation to seek justice to the victims of these Kind of atrocities. The Nations that ratified the Rome statute should refocus their objective and the same spirit that created the court is still needed and they should always stand with the court, if truly in their purpose, they had a positive objective.

The investigators would have done a better job and some areas needs an explanation on why such leads were not explored and either the Court should be empowered more or be an extension of the United Nations security council and be empowered with all powers that can be, to tame wild dogs in search of political power whose blood thirst ego force them to slaughter thousands and by stretching their thigh muscles they conspire and secretly position the court as irrelevant while they fail to offer alternatives.

Kenya government should had known the genesis of these clashes in 1992, were the Kalenjin community reacting to propaganda leaflets dropped by Mungiki members?

I honestly believe true Justice can never be realized in these world for some personalities or political policies are masters that rules and though they may be evil, they are allowed to tame other wild dogs like them. This is a witness account ,the unfolding events that begins with the formation of Mungiki, its roots to Mau Mau, secret oaths, political financing, their role in Kenya Political violence 2007/8 General Election, Uhuru Kenyatta, verdict of guilty or not guilty in the public court and failures of the International criminal Court to prosecute and investigate the case even though they had available lead of evidence that any serious investigator would have used to render justice to the victims of these atrocities, though it has a complex nature that needed to be traced.

 This book also points on significant spiritual similarities that will help the reader realize the mutation or transformations of spiritual influences.

In the spirit world we have only two source of influence, while one influence is God Spirit, The Holy Spirit which remains the same with the same attributes and character, the other source of spirit influence, mutates, transforms and assume all sort of character camouflaging to the ordinary eye but it's nature, it's true seed, is satanic, demonic manifestation of spiritual influence that struggles to fulfill prophetic caliphates and Kingdoms by enslaving, communities and individuals to serve an evil purpose.

CHAPTER   ONE:

WITNESS CREDIBILITY.

As stated in the introduction, I'm a Christian and my Judge is God, my life was preserved as a testimony, in actual sense I ought to have died and my memories forgotten probably only living within those that may have loved me, I owe great thanks and prayer to those that supported me, some had to pass on by standing with me, my family, friends, the faith led Mungiki defectors that were killed when they said No to Mungiki, my relatives and unknown sympathizers some who wouldn't understand why I had to face these ugly monsters, evil political forces in the government and in Mungiki.

I resigned from Beta Healthcare Int with an aim of facing the perpetrators of tribal clashes who I believed were in the government, I believed my actions and thought were God driven, I didn't understand why can't people speak truth and call a spade a spade, I didn't know some statements were hard to utter even though they were inscribed in one's heart. I didn't know life is a drama and sometimes you act as a fool and pretend you really don't understand, a path that is usually travelled by many quickening their steps to hell.

I didn't know I have entered into a life journey that I would witness a loss of many lives, who I came to know as friends, acquaintances and comrades, some agreeing with me and accepted truth, truth they only perceived in their mind and didn't know what lied ahead. If I had seen a trailer of this 'movie,' I wouldn't have been in it. I would have not made my first step to face these devils and monsters, a fact that is proven by my scare flights on two occasions.

When the Kikuyu-Mungiki prophet messenger was commissioned by the devil to manipulate through Kikuyu ancestral spirits or whatever authority or principality that commissioned him, with a message to the Kikuyus in preparation of the tribal clashes, The God of the Heavens, Savior of mankind Lord Jesus Christ also came to me in the same line of family and tribe that was to host and support the growth of Mungiki. There is always a light in any deep darkness, God always have a true witness, a testimony that would raise a voice declare God to be true, savior, protector and refuge to those who by his mercies had been directed to receive grace.

I was a sinner like any other, but God had chosen me at my late 20's to be exact on 3rd may 1991 and my encounter with Him left a permanent change that can never be undone.

In His mystery of the Holy Spirit, he came down and engulfed me within and out while in a prayer at my tiny one bedroomed house in Umoja one estate Nairobi, this was after I had asked him in prayer, 'which is the true church that would teach me about his ways, his reality and truth'?, I didn't know my prayer had reached the heart and purpose of God for before I finished my statement of prayer, I was on fire by the Holy Spirit, numb, and in an almost unconscious state, a scenario that only those that had that kind of experience can understand that experience. In the language of the scriptures it is called a second birth to the true seed, a circumcision of the heart, where one is given a new heart, a new mind, a new purpose of life and one life is 'germitized' to possess the life of God, eternal life, but not all becomes the seed of God, when the Holy Spirit falls on a wrong seed, as rain falls in the field, it is just as rain and as the seed in the heart germinates, the fruit is produced accordingly. The true seed, growing and believing the word of God, conquering all hypocrisy and manifesting Christ-like life.

I didn't know the true purpose of this lied in the future for there is nothing that God does without a purpose, he does all things for his glory as a testimony of his attributes and true Christians are called for a God driven purpose. A period of 9 years passed without realizing exactly what lied ahead though by a voice, God had talked to me while walking along a road that connects Jogoo rd. Nairobi and House of Manji Industrial Area Nairobi, I had had a conversation with the Almighty asking me what I wanted to do with my life and having directed by Him through His wisdom, I answered him "I want nothing except to do your will".

After The Holy Spirit baptism by fire experience, I concluded I'm called among the Pentecostals and therefore became a Pentecostal, a reference where early believers saw tongues of fire that fell to them in the upper room as quoted in the Bible. My mentors and teachers advised me that until I spoke in tongues, audible unknown or known tongues I'm not yet done, I needed that sign as a prove of The Holy Spirit Baptism, I prayed to God and sought those tongues until God gave me that gift.

My pastors and teachers of this Pentecostal experience were in error for tongues are not a sign of The Holy Spirit Baptism, [a lesson for another day] Pentecostal denominations have built their faith on that but is an error, a lesson I came to learn later through the unfolding spiritual journey that God had prepared for me. I became a Pentecostal follower and sojourned among them.

That voice that I had earlier heard while walking to work in Industrial area Nairobi came back and asked me to get prepared for that purpose, that God had intended for me, a command that I wouldn't have reasoned, questioned or answered back, it was very authoritative and scary. I obliged and resigned my work as a van salesman with Beta Healthcare Int, a decision among many such decisions perceived by rational thinkers as wrong, irresponsible and unwarranted, questioning the sanity of the victim, and by human reasoning they have an explanation in the study of mind called psychology.

Those trained in the ways of faith, whatever faith knows that faith led decisions have a degree of insanity to the normal ordinary minds.

Spiritual science is a very wide subject and humans are still trying to understand this science but there is only one genuine teacher of this subject and its study is prophetic, it lies within the time allotted for man to live in these globe and persons trained to soar high as eagles, can see past, present and future and do unlock the mystery of this science.

l also tried to rationalize my decision and later thought I was wrong, and I tried to interpret that encounter by honestly judging myself and analyzing the problems that I felt needed to be solved or tackled and as a victim of 1992 tribal clashes, I thought, "I'm directed to honestly speak against the evil called tribal clashes, corruption in the government and errors practiced and taught by church ministers who follow traditions of men and doctrines that are based on teachings that doesn't reflect Lord Jesus Christ ministry of the Bible days". I had analyzed many things and saw them wrong, I was seeking answers.

My heart and mind were free for a lesson, a lesson that I could only learn from God, I wasn't ready to learn from any other source having had an encounter with God, I was in his hands to shape me, teach me, train me and unlock the mystery of questions that lingered in my mind.

I was seeking an answer to unlock the life mystery, from governance to religion, from race, to tribes, life to death. Though I had had an encounter with God through The Holy Spirit Fire Baptism and had heard His Word, there stood a cloud of mystery that hang in the air and only through Him that Mystery could be solved, in my innocence I was in for a journey and a painful one, forsaking everything and riding on his wisdom, protection and power.

Armed in faith, believing God, I faced the monsters of evil that rules people hearts and enslave many, little did I know that, were it not for God who by foreknowledge had seen the devil creeping and prepared a testimony of himself, the monster was ready to swallow me and destroy my life. Praise God and Glory to name, He lives to testify of himself.

In that experience and having a right altitude, condemning none, loving all, enemies and friends alike, praying for all to came to the full knowledge of truth. My conscious is clear before men and God and God being my judge, I'm responding to the truth of being, the reality of light that rests in truth.

I cannot withhold truth or feel comfortable in the midst of blind people who are following a path that its destiny is everlasting hell, where tribal spirits, race, color religion and to an extend even nation spirits blinds humanity and fails to judge individuals on the basis of their character and as such innocent victims are in wholesale condemned, fought, burned in churches, houses torched and population displaced as witnessed in Kenya during 2007/8 tribal clashes. A whole population is manipulated by a devil, a HIDDEN mystery that only those trained in tracing weird deceit, lies can truly unlock such mysteries through the help of God and set the captives free.

At some moment of you reading this book, you may have judged me or already you are passing a judgement. Concepts, views and especially 'intellectual' based quick analysis falls short of grasping the core purpose or inner alignment of issues because intellectual understanding is mostly research based and my simple command of English language can be a hindrance to the likes of me who tries to interpret words in many languages before they are expressed, excuse me for that and simply understand that I'm struggling to pass a message typing with two or three fingers for in my school days computers were unknown and I haven't been in any computer class.

I'm struggling to make a point to express an experience as I saw it and witnessed. Not just as an analysis of what I experienced, No! I'm opening hidden rotten wounds that needs treatment, and use this as an awakening call to an avenue of study not to defeat evil by guns and bombs but to open some eyes to understand there exist only one source of true knowledge, one truth, I'm challenging learned political intellectuals who manipulate illiterate population to fight wars that are completely unnecessary instead of them leading to change humanity for better at least a step better.

These tribal, racial, religious caliphs, manipulate their subjects to kill one another in their selfish individual interests called politics, whose real goals are corruption, more corruption, murder, rape and all sorts of evil. Please slow down with me flash back, open more links in your mind, reflect as the story unfolds and grasp the story from a meditative point of view with a wider understanding of exactly what I'm leading to, my story is not my story, it is your story but probably from a different approach.

CHAPTER   TWO:

THE   FORMATION   OF MUNGIKI.

It would be a story with a missing a link, if I jump straight into writing how Mungiki begun without a background of its root, for every seed planted germinates and brings forth a fruit of its own kind, Kenya Republic was a colony of the British protectorate and in 12th December 1963, it gained its independence from the British with Jomo Kenyatta as its first president. Prior to this date of independence, there was a military outfit called the Mau Mau that was formed after the 2nd world war by soldiers that participated in that war. The most known name among the returnees and formation of this group was Dedan Kimathi who had actually had shown rebellion from a British commander after a racial remark.

The legend and freedom fighter Dedan Kimathi was Mau Mau Freedom Fighter captured and hanged by the British in 1957.

Mau Mau originated from the Kikuyu tribe in Kenya, though it had members from other tribes and the Agikuyu as a tribe had its own religion prior to the introduction of

Christianity by Christian missionaries and part of Kikuyu culture and customs went beyond just moral teachings but included political leadership and in every Kikuyu generation, a lineage of leadership known as "riika", a "ituika "change of guard takes place and in my generation it's was not exceptional,[these are the spirits that haunts] that resurrected with a messenger in my generation and being in the lineage of a clan of "ethaga", a lineage of oath administrators and in exact locations where the devils were sowing a seed of discord in a generation, I was also commissioned by God to learn and trace a seed as is it grows and testify to you how devils manipulate and enslave many.

 Some Mau Mau freedom fighters had settled in Olenguruone and had commissioned their struggle and oath taking ceremony in Olenguruone Molo sometimes in 1948 during the freedom struggle, a spirit from hell had set and chosen this place as a launching pad of its operation, a rebirth.

Mau Mau was ready for a rebirth with a new name Mungiki. Strange as it seems, my cousin David Waithaka Wagacha was the first youth who introduced Mungiki generation to take Mau Mau oath from the Mau Mau elders through an oath administrator called Mzee Kimamo Wanjohi, by then over 80 years old.

Mzee Kimamo Wanjohi is also believed by his own words to have administered the Mau Mau oath to Jomo kenyatta, the first president of Kenya in Olenguruone in 1948.

Historians doubt if actually Kenyatta was a Mau Mau, but Mau Mau wasn't an individual choice, it was a community clarion call to fight the British.

Moderate Kikuyus who had been influenced through Christian missionaries and western education thought that Kikuyu Mau Mau ritual was outdated and choose to be royal to the British, while others choose other means of struggle and Kenyatta was among this group, having said so, his activities does not alienate him from a fact that during his activities as a politician he may been trapped and cornered to take a Mau Mau oath and had no choice but secretly support Mau Mau.

Many may have not openly supported Mau Mau, the secret Mau Mau oath had been kept, a community dark evil that is not openly discussed, the scenario that unfolds in oath dens are not children bedtime stories.

The historians that defend Kenyatta position ought to explain why did he see it necessary to gather all Kikuyus, Meru and Embu communities in 1966 and take them to Gatundu his home for the famous "chai wa Kenyatta". Tea of Kenyatta.

The "chai" wa kenyatta was a Mau Mau oath ritual, binding the said communities to support and fight for Kenyatta government, Kenyatta had realized the Kenya People's Union [KPU] Odinga rebellion was taking a wrong path and he feared for a bloody confrontation, he gathered his community as traditions demand and gave them "chai", oath to defend their "caliphate, a perceived spiritual monarchy because of Oginga Odinga KPU Rebellion 1966.

Mau Mau actually was never formed to fight for Kenyan independence, "ithaka na wiyathi", land and freedom did not represent Kenya colony, it was about Kikuyu land and Kikuyu freedom. Freedom of Kenya colony was a responsibility for each tribe to demand their freedom, Kenya colony existed in the minds of the British and Kikuyu elites. Nearly all the Mau Mau militias were illiterate and their struggle was focused on their tribe alone," ithaka na wiyathi". They therefore encouraged other tribes to fight their own freedom like the Kisii and Mijikenda in the coast who they partnered with.

There is a wrong concept of history record had been written with a concept of the elites who misplaced Mau Mau as Kenya freedom fighters, there was no army, rebel group or Militia fighting for Kenya freedom, Mau Mau were fighting tribal Kingdoms and had no intention of ruling Kenya as a federal government, Kenya Colony or Kenya republic was in the eyes of the elites, the Kikuyu Mau Mau were fighting for a Kikuyu-"caliphate", a spiritual Kikuyu Kingdom but the Kikuyu intellectuals of the day benefited from whatever goals that Mau Mau had achieved by fighting the British. Mungiki formation and growth points to exactly in the same trend with Mau Mau, and the political elites using the same principles.

What these elites couldn't understand is a fact that a populace can be manipulated by a devil and they therefore agreed to partner with Mau Mau to achieve a certain objective in a most cruel method called traditional oath, a repetitive occurrence was ready to trap them again through Mungiki.

 Each and every clan of the Kikuyu tribe was positioned for a particular service to the tribe, two clans were involved in leadership and priesthood, "Ambui" and "Ethaga",I was born from the priesthood clan of "ethaga" and I'm told my great grandfather Ndungu Wananu Waithaka was actually a respected oath administrator, a priest and in that lineage my cousin Charles Ndungu Wagacha inherited that 'anointing' and was the head of Mungiki oath administration passed over to him by a Mau Mau general and oath administrator called Mzee Kimamo Wanjohi.

My cousin didn't learn that his great grandfather was an oath administrator and therefore went to seek it as an inheritance but by lineal descent of positioning that defines our being through birth, this unfolded almost as a naturally occurrence. He was imprisoned in that call of duty for the tribe of the Kikuyu and when times called for his service, blinded and enslaved through birth he had no options for other options required a rebirth a spiritual phenomenal that had not awakened in him, he didn't understand it.

Our lineal descent, no matter how seen to have a godly attribute, is of the devil, the traditional doctrines and practices are for the purpose of manipulation by demonic spirits that enslaves and blind it's subjects into miserable lives serving masters of evil.

I also through the same lineage of birth, this spiritual lineage haunted me and demanded my service in that lineage of the "ethaga", but by the grace of God before the real encounter with the messenger who happens to be also a distant cousin from the clan of "Ambui"[John Maina Kamunya also known as Maina Njenga]The spiritual leader of

Mungiki sent to awaken this service, I had already experienced a spiritual rebirth and therefore, my soul and spirit were not available though forcefully I was given the kikuyu oath of service through whipping while completely naked and forced to undergo a ritual of oath taking in a most inhuman way that I had never experienced before or encountered and my prayer is, may I not die in the hands of my enemies. That was and is always my prayer.

God allowed me through my weaknesses as human being by fear of death and the purpose of bringing to light things done in darkness to undergo all these not one oath but twice I was forcibly humiliated to take these oaths, threatened with death for refusal to obey the commands, no one is spared once trapped and cornered to take these oaths and sometimes either through resistance or uncontrolled beating some don't make it and are killed, body parts dismembered and disposed without trace.

These rituals are passed through generation to generation and when in my generation, when the lineage of the ancestral spirits demanded that our service was required, thousands of Kikuyu youths were not spared and for the purpose of research and knowledge, one need to refer to a Kikuyu seer Mugo Kibiru, Mugo wa Kibiru Prophesy before the coming of the British and colonizing Kenya.

This Kikuyu seer prophesied about dominance by the white man rule in Kikuyu land-not Kenya], dominance of the White man in Kikuyu land.

Kenya colony was a British creation it never existed in the mind concept of this Kikuyu seer, neither did it exist among the kikuyus. Kikuyu tribe had their own way of governance and Mugo Kibiru saw a dominance that led to a struggle that created a Kikuyu "caliphate"- an ethnic spiritual Kingdom. Why a caliphate? The ruler that was to come was anointed by the Kikuyu tradition rituals, the Mau Mau Kikuyu tradition rituals that Kenyatta rode on to became the first President of Kenya.

Kikuyus perception of a "Muthamaki", King was considered spiritual and to an extent even today among many. Though Kenyatta was voted as the president of Kenya, he was a tribal" caliph" of an Ethnic-Kingdom.

He outwitted his peers and rode on tribal kinsmen ignorance who didn't understand a struggle beyond their land, Dedan Kimathi having been educated understood this fact, retraced his steps and was on the way to surrender before he was captured, he had fully realized that his Kikuyu Militia Mau Mau had no hope of having an Independent ethnic caliphate outside the bigger Kenya colony.

The struggle of the Kikuyu tribe for their land and freedom, "ithaka na wiyathi" [Ref further link for research -Imperial Reckoning: The Untold Story of Britain's Gulag in Kenya] -.meaning land and freedom, recapture of political power from the British and freedom restored with a Kikuyu as "Muthamaki" King, was prophesied by Mugo Kibiru and it came to pass with Jomo Kenyatta inaugurated as the first President of Kenya on 12th December 1963.Mugo Kibiru had also prophesied the political power shifting base and taken by another tribe.

In 1978 after Jomo Kenyatta death, the Kalenjin tribe took political power through the 2nd President of the Republic of Kenya Daniel Arap Moi. The seer had also seen tribal clashes that was to follow for the mantle of political leadership to be handed back to the Kikuyu tribe again, strangely as it seems Mugo Kibiru having lived in the 18th and early 19th century his prophesy unfolded as told, unconsciously or consciously each player fulfilling these prophecies.

Who were these Players? WHO IGNITED THESE CLASHES? DID THE KALENJIN PLAN THE TRIBAL CLASHES TO EVICT KIKUYUS IN 1992?

Kenya was created by the British, tribes existed as Kingdoms and ethnic nations that had their own system of governance, they had borders and conflicts. When the struggle for independence started, it was not a struggle of a nation called Kenya, No! but tribal nations, kingdoms-ethnic "caliphates". Mau Mau was born along these lines and Mugo Kibiru prophecy was on this line of an ethnic Kikuyu Kingdom, a belief among many Kikuyus.

What many fail to see in Mugo Kibiru prophecy, is that he also spoke of an ethnic-kingdom in reference to "Uthamaki ndukoima ringi Nyumba ya Mumbi" this mantle of leadership likened to a monarchy in the house of Mumbi will never again depart from Mumbi house and strangely enough the son of the first President of Kenya Uhuru Kenyatta took presidency from another Kikuyu Mwai kibaki. Kikuyus considers themselves to be from one house, one family." Nyumba ya Mumbi'. ARE KIKUYUS TIED TO THIS BOND OF ETHNIC ENSLAVEMENT?

In one of these prophetic events during the changeover of the political mantle of leadership as Mugo Kibiru prophesy, the shedding of blood was witnessed and Uhuru kenyatta from "Ambui" clan son of a Kikuyu seer continues to fulfill this prophesy. One can have a different outlook but without a tribal support Uhuru Kenyatta had no politics or leadership qualities that would have made him a president neither do William Ruto, they rode on tribal roots and ignorance of their subjects.

Politics in Kenya has nothing to do with the Kenya that the British created, it is a hybrid nation that it's citizen are yet to realize it, politics is about tribal ethnic nations and no president has ever come out of these ethnic kingdoms and shown any statesmanship of the hybrid nation.

Strange prophetic events, Uhuru trailed on the same tracks, with a tag accused as his father with charges of crimes committed against humanity in the International criminal court in The Hague Netherlands.

Maina Njenga, the Mungiki leader originated from Nyahururu, Karandi Laikipia West, in the final year of his 'O Level education-form four', he was unable to do his examination because of supernatural spiritual influence that made him behave weird, he was later taken to a Muslim medium who performed a ritual that stabilized him. He came prophesying on the same line of as Mugo Kibiru talking of a "kirinyaga Kingdom" likened to an Islamic caliphate.

The same line of manipulation awakening the tribe in the lineal descent of a kingdom and establish a monarch-caliphate.

 In the early 1989, Maina Njenga having been commissioned by these Kikuyu ancestral spirits and undergone a ritual to awaken these spirits [strange enough not from another Kikuyu but a Somali reciting the Koran], he had travelled from Nakuru to Molo in Rift Valley province of the Republic of Kenya and he came prophesying of ethnic war that was to take place in Rift valley by then Mungiki existed only in a spiritual world and only in word.

In the spirit world devils are all the same, they manipulate people though principalities, [Prince Demons] that rule Nations, tongues, tribes and people, religious rituals associated to these devils, demons and diverse tribal rituals all plan pointing to one thing, enslaving and to blind humanity not to understand Truth, which is the word of God and having only one source The Bible.

This demon spirit later referred by Islamic scholars as "Jinn", came in a line of a prophesy following the same steps used to radicalize youths in Islamic faith, manipulating it's subject to believe a prophecy and hang on a doctrine of lineal descent to establish a caliphate.

Maina Njenga would use the word Mungiki meaning multitude but not specifically an organization and he would say," I have seen a multitude of people engaged in ethnic war, carcasses of the dead people were scattered everywhere", "dead bodies", "dead bodies" everywhere". He came to Molo in Rift valley preaching about this strange war that was to unfold, this formed the basis, the foundation of the resurrection of the Mau Mau in a new generation.

 My cousin David Waithaka Wagacha met Maina Njenga while he was going home from a school known as Njenga Karume secondary school in Molo, he was in form three by then and while walking home from school where he lived with my aunt, a sister of my father,' Grace Wangari Waithaka', he encountered a gathering of people listening to a strange looking fellow prophesying strange happenings that would unfold, the eviction of Kikuyu tribe from the Rift valley. Curious to know more about the events and prophecy, he invited Maina Njenga to my aunt's place where David was living and this was the first encounter with Maina Njenga and my relatives in Molo Rift Valley.

David didn't have a clue that Maina Njenga was also his cousin, it was just out of curiosity that somehow he invited Maina Njenga to his home, his maternal aunt also an aunt of Maina Njenga had previously helped Maina Njenga parents seek a medium to help them treat Maina Njenga who had occasionally been taken ill and Doctors were unable diagnose his illness, this prompted them to seek a medium who happened to be a Somali Muslim who used the Koran verses in reciting his oracle. devils have no boundaries.

Maina Njenga was commissioned through this Islamic ritual by a Muslim medium reciting Koran verses, which were written in a piece of paper in Arabic. The written Koran verses were cut into small pieces, put on a glass with water and the contents were stirred. Maina was ordered to drink.

This was to commission the Prince demon of a" caliphate" nature, Islamic Koranic spirit, the spirit that sowed seeds witnessed only similar to what Isis are doing in the middle east and North Africa. Maina Njenga controlled Mungiki as a prophet-'Jinn', a king -Caliph and his authority was absolute.

Koran have verses that prophesy of establishing of Islamic caliphate which is used to propagate Jihad teaching, Caliphate prophecy, a seed of prophesy to a people who have faith in that prophetic writing or prophecy is a prime ground ready to sow seeds based on that ideology, the entire Muslim world is a fertile ground for Caliphate ideology, the prophecy in the Koran and the timing, waters that kind of seed and it germinates. Kikuyu tribe had a prophecy that was waited to unfold but Christianity influence, western culture and education had changed their ways of life, though still holding on certain values that identify them as a tribe.

Tribal roots, race or religion sometimes is a mystery that many wish to discover, their origin and uniqueness and when a prophetic message that has a backing of a distant past of accepted authority, i.e. oral prophecy passed through generation to generation or written writings considered inspired, then a ground is already cultivated to sow seeds based on that Kind of prophecy.

DID MAINA NJENGA WENT TO RIFT VALLEY TO IGNITE THE TRIBAL CLASHES AND FULFILL THE PROPHECY?

Maina Njenga popularity had grown due to cleansing ceremonies he would perform that claimed to heal certain diseases, and in so doing many believed in him including my aunt and as a result, my aunt offered Maina Njenga shelter and her house was established as a base in Rift valley a launching pad for the future growth of the organization.

Rumors' spread all over, through PROPAGANDA, LEAFLETS and the "HEALINGS" and THROUGH THIS prophesy of tribal clashes that was to take place, he asked people to be cleansed through a ritual that was performed with water, incense and almond oil as a way of protecting themselves, by this time, some committed followers who later turned to be the backbone of Mungiki had taken heed of the message and became Maina associates. A few such people were Njoroge Wacucu, Maina cousin Ndura Waruinge who turned be Mungiki National coordinator, my cousin David Waithaka Wagacha, Njoroge Wacucu mother and my aunt Grace Wangari Waithaka.

The prophecy continued in the greater Rift valley area, Kericho, Eldoret and Nakuru and Maina Njenga was introduced to my relatives in Kericho and Eldoret, he visited Eldoret asking my relatives also to undergo this ritual of water cleansing as a means of protection from their enemies, he had by now rooted himself as a prophet with a divine message. DURING THIS VISIT, MAINA NJENGA DISTRIBUTED PROPAGANDA LEAFLETS WARNING KIKUYUS OF EVICTION.

Messengers, caliphs, false prophets or leaders of these kind of prophesies, are individuals who are inspired from other forces from the world of spirits, their wits are beyond normal and are masters of lies and deceit, Maina Njenga used propaganda to speed up his prophecy, they would write materials and distribute them at night, alerting people of danger to come, they used to call them scuds. They would incite either party, targeted victims of their prophecy to prove a point, as David narrates "Maina Njenga followers would burn Kalenjin houses inciting the Kalenjin to react or vice versa".

MAINA NJENGA PLANTED A SEED TO FULFILL HIS PROPHECY BY TARGETING HIS INNOCENT VICTIMS AND LEAVING THEM TO FIGHT ONE ANOTHER.

In 1990 Maina Njenga came with a new message that he had been instructed by god to look for Mau Mau elders who were to help them to understand how they would encounter these tribal clashes that were about to unfold and they started enquiring where to meet these Mau Mau elders and as mentioned earlier by fate or positioning, these Mau Mau elders were within their vicinity and after enquires they were led to a Mau Mau General called Maina Mathara in Olenguruone Molo as David continues.

"We went to Olenguruone to see General Maina Mathara who took us also to Kuresoi and met Major General Hitler Eloto Okire, who happened to be from the Turkana tribe but circumcised and initiated as a Kikuyu and had joined Mau Mau during the freedom struggle. Major General Hitler told us, we have to look for other Mau Mau generals, a journey that was to take us to Muranga to see General Mwangi Kamau, a former Kikuyu Central Association official, who would be the lead man to gather other Mau Mau generals".

"We therefore left to Muranga to see General Mwangi Kamau, we left in the company of Major General Hitler, General Maina Mathara, I David Wagacha, Maina Njenga, his father Stephen kamunya and brother John Kamunya, former Mungiki National Coordinator Ndura Waruinge and Njoroge "Wacucu". General Mwangi Kamau told us he had to contact other Mau Mau generals like General Manegene from Meru, General Muthoni Kagotho from Embu and others, he told us that he need also to contact other Mau Mau Generals from Kisii region like General Nyanchama and Major Babu Ondari."

"The Muranga General Mwangi Kamau sent us to pick these Kisii generals and brought them to Muranga, we were also instructed to gather other Mau Mau generals among the

Mijikenda who were inspired by Mekatilili wa Menza during the freedom struggle and had a similar call".

"We therefore went to coast province contacted the Mijikenda elders who introduced us to the Mijikenda generals and we all met in Muranga under the guidance of General Mwangi Kamau".

 This link with Mau Mau generals among the Mijikenda awakened the same spirit among the Giriama, Digo and Taita communities, clashes were witnessed in the coast province of Kenya in 1997 and by fate or destiny I was in Mtwapa Mombasa Kenya working with Beta healthcare Int, formerly Boots company Plc as a pharmaceutical van salesman Mombasa region. when these clashes started.

I witnessed the resurrection of the spirit in the Coast province where many youths also underwent a ritual demanding separation from Kenya saying "Pwani si Kenya", Coast is not Kenya, they wanted a Kingdom of their own and today, Mombasa revolutionary council [MRC]is still a threat to Kenya National security.

STRANGE -TRIBAL CLASHES WERE NOT WITNESSED IN RIFT VALLEY IN 1997, MUNGIKI DIDN'T DISTRIBUTE THE PROPAGANDA LEAFLETS IN RIFT VALLEY IN 1997.

After the Muranga Mau Mau general's meeting, David continues" it was agreed, 'we write a letter to the President of Kenya by then President Daniel Moi, so that the President would help us mobilize all Mau Mau generals countrywide, it was agreed that since Mau Mau had a council that was recognized by the Kenya government, it would be wise to use that banner, The Kenya ex-war council KANU elders, a Mau Mau war council of elders that had been formed under the guidance of the first President Jomo Kenyatta ,as a patriotic movement to support the Kenya government".

"We therefore wrote a letter to the president requesting him to urgently mobilize all the living Mau Mau generals for a meeting with him in Nakuru State house, I David Wagacha wrote the letter which was stamped with the Kenya ex-war council KANU elders' official rubber stamp seal and within three days, the Provincial administration had been mobilized to pick all Mau Mau generals for a Meeting with The President in Nakuru state house, a meeting that was held on December 23 1991".

"In the meeting, which was convened for the purpose to officially mandate the youth to preach patriotism, it was agreed that the Mau Mau will have one of their own to represent them in Parliament and the youth be allowed to hold meetings to preach patriotism".

I personally met Maina Njenga in Molo in 1991 while working in the North Rift Valley Region as a pharmaceutical salesman with Boots Company Plc and in my itinerary as a salesman, I had decided to visit my aunt home where Maina was residing and he tried to preach to me to accept his message of prophesies and believe in Kikuyu culture and customs, which he claimed were the basis of faith on the new dawn as he had been directed to preach about a return to our roots, our customs and culture.

I rejected his ideas turned him down and testified my faith in Lord Jesus Christ as a born again Christian, by then oath taking had not started and it was unknown to them, the only ritual he performed was a water cleansing ceremony likened to baptism, sprinkling of water as a means of protection, incense burning and use of almond oil. His fame through propaganda, leaflets circulation and the healings he claimed to perform had spread reaching the surrounding Kikuyu farming communities.

David recalls, "in 1992 general election his 'prophecies' unfolded, he sent some Mungiki Members to burn Kalenjin houses in NJORO, KIHINGO, RIKIA AND ELBURGON AREA". Whether this ignited the spread of the clashes or the Kalenjin were prepared for clashes due to EARLIER PROPAGANDA LEAFLETS, THAT CAN ONLY BE ANSWERED BY THE KALENJIN. The propaganda leaflets were demanding KANU had to change to KNC, BY DR NJOROGE MUNGAI".

Did the former president Daniel Moi and his Kalenjin Kinsmen fall in a trap set by Maina Njenga calling himself DR Njoroge Mungai who was demanding KANU TO CHANGE TO KNC, did these leaflets create worry and fear that sowed the seed of tribal clashes?

However, his prophecies unfolded, the start of the tribal clashes in the first Multiparty election in Kenya that challenged and demanded a change of guard in the Kenya politics, a challenge that was encountered with violent political influenced tribal clashes between the Kalenjin tribe which Daniel Moi, the then Kenya President belonged and the Kikuyu tribe whose front runner in the opposition Kenneth Matiba was perceived to be the main challenger to take the mantle of political leadership from Moi.

"The Kalenjin were fully armed and had prepared themselves for the tribal clashes, they were armed with imported arrows from Korea. [who armed them]? MOI colonies either had fallen in the trap and thought

Kikuyu were out to topple the government in the event of defeat in the 1992 general election or through skeptical fear they were out to create chaos

I was born in Kericho and my entire youth life, our home was in Eldoret, my closest friends as I grew up were Kalenjin, in teen life and as a young secondary school student. At one time, at the age of 11 years, I was rescued by a Kalenjin man at very late hours in the evening while trekking a distance of close to 30 kilometers to home, he took me to his house where I was fed and slept, 'was this not a soul sent by God to remind me at this hour', these people are not that evil, In my secondary days, Kalenjin friends welcomed me several times to share with me their food, I hate to believe, they can't do the same today, they never saw me and labelled me a Kikuyu or did I, at any one time feel unsafe with them. My father closest friend I had known in my teen life was a Kalenjin who owned a shop in Kipkaren Turbo- Mr. Memba Misoi. The seed of discord came from an ideology planted by a devil masquerading as an angel.

 As the tribal clashes progressed, "Maina Njenga told us he had a new message and had been instructed by god in a to seek help from the Mau Mau and enquire 'what is "Mungore activity" the 'libakusitu shwalingateku' [which means we should not let anyone divide us]."as David continues, "we enquired from the Mau Mau about what is "Mungore activity" and the Mau Mau elders told us it was taking oath to bind the community and establishing an the Kikuyu army, a process that neither Maina Njenga or any of us youths had known, and before any one of us youth had been initiated in this "Mungore activity "Maina Njenga had fled the clashes and was in Nairobi"{Note the Mode of operation],Ignite and flee.

"The clashes had taken an ugly face we were ill prepared unlike our aggressors the Kalenjin. While I and other youths were guarding our farms, unaware what lied ahead, a step that would change Kenya history and give birth to a dreaded militia outfit was already a seed preparing to germinate, little did I know that among the youths with me my friend D.O Kamau Mwathi and My mother who was in our homestead in this abnormal evening our fate had been decided, an abnormal evening was darkening, abnormal in the sense that it turned to be the day I was given the Mau Mau oath and a journey begun "David said..

"We had been marked, as some church elders came at night led by a local Catholic church chairman, elder Peter Kamau,' a person who I knew and who happened to be my godfather in my earlier baptism ceremony in a local catholic church', he approached me and told me that 'we were invited to take a cup tea in a local elder house where they were planning how to protect ourselves' and since this was a person who of course I trusted as an elder I had no question back in my mind to think any kind of misfortune, mistrust or otherwise, I went with him to a local elder house called Mr. Kahanya and immediately I entered the house, my fate was sealed".

"They started whipping me ,'telling me 'remove your clothes, remove all of them', this confused me, thinking why are they doing this to me yet I'm a man like them, I thought they think I'm uncircumcised and I complained' I'm a man' but they continued whipping me telling me "uyu ni thingira wa gikuyu", this is the house of Mumbi, "house of Mumbi" meaning the origin of the tribe as it is believed Mumbi was the mother of all the Kikuyus" ."This is the preparation of kikuyu army militia, they told me, the ritual here is "giathi kia guhaa ni gutu" [the ritual here is listening], so they whipped me and naked as I was born, I was forced to go round a ritual altar seven times, swearing that I will never reveal the secrets of the community and if I reveal what is happening here, 'may this oath kill me, if I reveal this, may this goat kill me', [oath taking ceremony is normally taken by a sacrificial goat].So I was forced to take this oath swearing seven times to be a Kikuyu army militia". "This oath was the same Mau Mau oath for "ithaka na wiyathi, protecting Kikuyu land. The oath is not about Kenya but Kikuyu land, and freedom of Kikuyu".

 "This was the kikuyu Mau Mau conspiracy that linked us the youth to the traditional Mau Mau oath and as the community was 'under threat', this ritual was already taking place initiated by the community itself and from that point, one is enslaved to that oath, a mental slavery that binds you to the community and refusal, denial or defection means death".

 The devil had grounded himself, the Kikuyu communities in the larger Molo, Nakuru and Eldoret area were caught in a surprise, WERE THESE KIKUYUS VICTIMS OF THE SAME SEED OF EVIL PLANTED BY MUNGIKI THROUGH MAINA NJENGA BY MANIPULATION.

 "I David was trained by these Mau Mau elders how to handle guns, homemade rifles and Kikuyu traditional militia training. I was instructed to decoy my mother, other neighbors' and youths through invitation to take tea in one of this Kikuyu elders house for this Kikuyu traditional oath".

Custodians of any particular tribe are the elders that performs specific rituals that identify and protect that tribe, language doesn't make one to belong to particular tribe, not all Kikuyus can claim to be elders because of age and speaking Kikuyu, though a community can change and develop new culture and values.

The kikuyu elders by their knowledge of community guarded secrets, passed on a ritual to a younger generation authenticating themselves as custodians of Kikuyu culture and customs, a conspiracy and a fact that can be denied by the moderate changed community.

Seeds have their properties in their original form, a hybrid seed cannot reproduce an original seed, whatever has been hybridized cannot claim an original propensity of an original seed, no matter how human hybrid themselves, through change of culture, values and etc., they cannot be of different species, they remain rooted in evil, they need a new life, a new birth from the creator himself.

Kikuyu community like any other community, tribe, tongues, race or nation have undergone a change through the influence of Christianity, education and etc. but their roots is subconsciously buried in their original seed, the seed of their ancestors who lived in a "Caliphate" kind of a Kingdom, they try to hybrid, modernize themselves but their actions, political practices, traditions and the clarion call in times of wars or unexplained human encounters betrays them, they quickly goes to their shells and conspire accepting to redefine themselves as "nyumba ya Mumbi".

This happens in any community, race, tribe or nation, and all have a very dark history, barbaric. primitive practices that carry all sort of evil. Hypocrisy becomes the order that creates acceptance, denying the truth of God, that one need a complete new life, a new seed, a seed from God. Humans development religion, modernization, civilization, education and everything combined with it has proven that humans possess in their deep subconscious a seed that is manipulated to mutate, and transforms itself as a hybrid seed, an evil seed whose origin binds them in their race, color, religion or tribe and at some time to their shame, the evil seed in them manifests.

A story of shame as David continues," the tribal clashes progressed and the elders realized we were ill equipped with homemade guns, machetes and lacking all necessary tools to counter these attacks, i.e. guns, ammunition logistics support and financial help, I was therefore instructed with other Kikuyu Mau Mau elders to go to Nairobi, in the capital city to gather support by giving oath to the community in Nairobi".

"We needed money, we needed guns and the support of the community. A 'former air force captain' by the name of Njuguna Ngengi "captain GG", [killed during clashes], and General Maina Mathara were sent to see Hon Njenga Karume, 'former minister defense', GEMA Chairman [Gikuyu, Meru, Embu Association] and as a youth, who was now more experienced, I also accompanied these elders for a mission to recruit more people and seek support from the wider Kikuyu community, by then I was a Major now in the Kikuyu militia army".

"We arrived in Nairobi and set an oath den in Dandora Estate in Nairobi, General Kimamo Wanjohi who had also arrived in Nairobi was the oath administrator where I personally lured Maina Njenga, my brothers Charles Ndungu, and others for this Mau Mau oath, in fact I was a guard in the oath ceremony done now in Nairobi by Mau Mau generals".

"After Maina Njenga was given oath, he immediately told us that, 'that was what he referred as "Mungore activity" and he was so happy about it, he told us this work now, the oath administration process should not be left to the elders, they were slow and old', one of them General Kimamo told us that he is the one who administered the Mau Mau oath to the first president Jomo Kenyatta".

"We asked him if we can be trained as oath administrators and he confidently told us so long one is 18 years old and circumcised, one can practice how to administer these Kikuyu oaths".

"Mzee Kimamo Wanjohi the Mau Mau General asked us for volunteers for the oath administration training and my brother, Charles Ndungu Wagacha and D.O Kamau Mwathi volunteered and they became the first youths to take the mantle of elders as oath administrators', I David Waithaka Wagacha became an instructor to the new initiates".

"After our training how to slaughter the goats, collecting other paraphernalia used for the oath ceremony and having now a full blessing of the elders, we took our own goat and prepared a Kikuyu altar and performed a "ituika", change of guard and we lured these elders now demoting them as junior recruits by performing the same ritual administering the same oath to them and from that time the Mau Mau mantle was transferred to their children the youth of our generation"." The elders now went back to the villages to rest as by now the mantle had been handed over".

"The youth had now become the Mau Mau and since the message here was to form a multitude we referred ourselves as Mungiki a kikuyu word meaning multitude. These were first steps of the Kikuyu conspiracy that secretly kept the Mungiki alive in the steps of their forefathers, the Mau Mau and in 1993 Mau Mau became Mungiki".

"We were not an entity separate from the Mau Mau David said, 'as many believed or a religious organization whose sole aim was to practice traditional rituals, we were fully recruited by the Mau Mau, supported by the Mau Mau, with the community blessings and received a blessing to protect and prepare the Kikuyu army militia whose aim was community political interests, to protect "ithaka na wiyathi" land and freedom. Our caliphate-kingdom as Mugo wa Kibiru prophesy".

"Mungiki grew and new recruits initiated as Kikuyu Militias and after word went around within the Kikuyu community that kikuyus were preparing for a takeover of political power and preparing to protect the community interests, we met one famous kikuyu traditional worshipper called Ngonya Wa Gakonya who introduced us to Hon Ngengi Muigai 'former M.P Gatundu' a cousin to The president of Kenya Uhuru Kenyatta at his office in Bruce house

Nairobi, Hon Ngengi Muigai was very happy to meet us and after a brief introduction, he welcomed us and offered support by donating three cars for us, two saloon car a Nissan cedric, a Toyota trueno and Nisan Van, He also decided to introduce his friends to us Hon Captain Njeru Gathangu, 'former M.P Runyenjes' and Hon David Murathe 'former M.P Gatanga' all of them were very happy and being a bit elderly they encouraged us telling us they all waited these prophesy to fulfill and quoted Mugo Kibiru, the Kikuyu prophet of the 18th century".

"Other opposition leaders were also introduced to us, Hon George Nyanja, 'former M.P Limuru' and David Mwenje, 'former M.P Embakasi Nairobi' among others, we lured them one by one and we gave them oaths and many of them encouraged us, supported us and told us these was the only means of removing the then President from Daniel Arap Moi from power, some donated money, some guns with, Hon Paul Muite giving four G3 rifles".

"At one time with the help of Hon David Murathe, Hon George Nyanya and Hon David Mwenje, we decoyed other opposition M.Ps to Village Inn in Kiambu, a hotel owned by Hon Njenga Karume and we administered the Kikuyu ritual oath close to 23 members of parliament, Hon David Murathe being one of the guards with a G3 rifle in this ritual ceremony having been given the oath earlier, he helped us keep the police at bay after the police patrol car came around the hotel while we were administering these oaths to his fellow M.Ps, who were naked and squating". One can check You-Tube.23 politicians on a Mungiki video.

"The village Inn saga raised eyebrows after one of the M.P complained to the then President Daniel Arap Moi and Hon Njenga Karume being a close friend to the president called us and inquired what had happened, we told him all what had happened, telling him, 'we were just being patriotic citizens engaging in community activities and the president knew about it having met him earlier and allowed us to preach patriotism during the Dec 23 1991 ex-war council KANU elders meeting in state house Nakuru', though off course the president hadn't given us a license to administer oaths" .

"Hon Njenga Karume satisfied with our answer arranged our second visit to see the then President Daniel Arap Moi, though by his own intelligent Moi knew something was cropping up among the Kikuyu community"." This incident had happened after the 1992 tribal clashes, Moi had won the election but the campaigns to prepare the Kikuyu Army Militias had continued, the opposition Kikuyu MPs, Kikuyu church leaders had now backed this process after realizing that serious problems lie in the future and at some time, a Kikuyu had to take the political mantle from the incumbent and unless the tribe got prepared tribal clashes may turn to be a storm whose wind maybe unstoppable".

"A rumor existed that was confirmed by Daniel Arap Moi that his intention was to hand power to the son of the first President of Jomo Kenyatta, Hon Uhuru kenyatta, who by then had tried to vie for Gatundu parliamentary seat but lost"." The 1992 tribal clashes formed the foundation and growth of Mungiki, the clashes prepared the community and though it is widely believed that Kikuyus in Rift valley were able to defend themselves from the Kalenjin Militias, that's far than truth, many Kikuyus fled, some lost their farms, some sold them at throw away prices".

"Many kikuyus fled Molo area and within its vicinity, the greater Eldoret area and Kericho, we were unable to withstand the Kalenjin warrior's prowess and preparedness, we fled and left our homes". "The wider Kikuyu community was not very ready for this war ,it's progression to civilization, Christian believes and believe in the rule of law was a hindrance to gather the community and to support the kikuyu traditional rituals in the making of Kikuyu army Militias, some youths after being initiated and oath administered to them disappeared completely and moved from their locality, they shunned the "batoni" meetings, platoon meetings and if it weren't for the support of powerful kikuyu personalities, especially the politicians the growth of Mungiki would have been slow and heart breaking exercise. Propaganda leaflets kept Mungiki alive, Mungiki existed and positioned itself through fear and from the year 2000 to 2007, the monster it had created itself was bigger than its real image".

"Maina Njenga authority in Mungiki was unquestionable he had established himself as a caliph- a king and a prophet those who tried to question his authority were labeled yellow star and marked to die"." Hon David Murathe had thought they could do a coup in Mungiki and tried to influence some Mungiki members to start another splinter group and challenge Maina Njenga, that splinter group headed by a Mungiki leader whose name was "Wakadush" were all killed or disappeared, Maina could not entertain dissidents".

"In another incident Maina Njenga had sexually assaulted a Mungiki girl normally referred as "redi" meaning bride, who accused him to other Mungiki members of rape, and according to Mungiki rules, when one faces such an accusation, the punishment was 25 strokes of cane while naked, Mungiki Members who heard the case gave Maina Njenga the sentence 25 strokes of cane naked, all were hunted down and killed, Maina Njenga was a caliph-a king and could summon any bride to marry her or be his concubine as he wished".

"He ruled and conquered he had already established his own caliphate among his fellow Kikuyus, he called it "Kirinyaga kingdom", whose mode of execution of its enemies within and out was by, beheading and dismemberment of body parts".

CHAPTER THREE:

MY INVOLVEMENT WITH MUNGIKI.

As mentioned earlier, my relatives the sons of my uncle, a brother to my father were the Mungiki leaders, in an African context a son of your brother father is your brother and due to the fact that many of my relatives were living in Rift valley, we were all victims of tribal clashes and long before I knew what was happening, they were already engaged in this wars from a tribal platform.

I came to them from a different line of thought, I had not heard their interest in vying for political seats and to me the tribal animosity called tribal clashes could only be handled through open, truthful dialogue within the laws of the land agreed as the basis of solving political issues that influence our co-existence as communities of different tribes, I therefore suggested to them an option for them as youths challenging the crop of Kikuyu leaders who seemed to be silent while the then President Daniel Moi and his colonies were fueling and supporting this tribal clashes in Rift valley as I thought.

 My suggestion immediately created a name for me within their circles and they called me" Mheshimiwa", Swahili meaning Honorable, my suggestion was," we completely dislodge the then Kikuyu leadership by starting an early campaign against them and offering an alternate leadership, I suggested we form a different political party to completely alienate the crop of leaders who I felt had let us down, that was a thinking" of an amateur in the field of political dirty waters.

I was decoyed by Maina Njenga to accompany him to Thika, Kiandutu slums and address the youth on the new political idea, but this turned to be a trap set in a location code named"02", where feared aggressive Mungiki adherents were administering Mungiki oaths to new recruits.

We arrived in Thika in two different cars and a guard who had been assigned to me took me to a gathering of some youths who had gathered in a small shanty structure waiting for Maina Njenga, I was introduced to the youth by Maina himself but I did not address the young men gathered there as our plans.

We left this shanty structure and Maina rode on a bicycle to a different location which I came to learn later as the "thingira wa gikuyu" house of Mumbi. A scout was sent to call me and after arriving in a compound where some women, young men and children seemed to have been enjoying a meal, a normal looking homestead, I was ushered in a room where I had been invited to pick a piece meat ,inside the room, I was shown a door to the right side and as I entered, a scene like for' hungry dogs' that had not been fed for a long time waited for me, whips and all kind of threats were in the air, inside a dark room with no windows, whips started raining on me, and with whispers I was told, "uyu ni thingira wa Gikuyu, guku twaragia na mehiho" ,this is house of Mumbi, we speak whispering here"," remove your clothes, remove your clothes", these were endless commands that continued, whips and all kinds of threats from every direction.

I was told Dedan Kimathi, the legend Mau Mau hero passed through this altar and every tribe have their own altar and I should obey or else I face the consequence which means death, I obliged without any second thought. In a reflex, I realized unless I agree with their demands, these primitive tribal kinsmen are going to kill me. None of my close relative were in this den even Maina Njenga himself was nowhere to be seen.

I went round an arc shaped altar adorned with all sort of garden paraphernalia seven times with whips still raining on me, naked, humiliated in a scenario beyond words and after squatting down facing an oath administrator, I was forced to repeat these words," if I reveal this oath, may this oath kill me, If I reveal what had happened here may this goat Kill me", at every statement I was forced to bite a piece of goat meat or sheep, which I later came to learn was dried uncooked meat. There were other several commands like," If I would be sent to bring the head of somebody considered an enemy of our course, I will obey without question, even if it's of my father, mother or relative"," I swear to defend the community land and freedom" ithaka na wiyathi". These statements of oath were seven in total.

After these rituals, one becomes a Mungiki but to me that was far than truth, I was given instructions not to bath for seven days and to hide my clothes I had put on until seven days were over.

I took a hot bath immediately I was home that evening, nursed the marks of the whips and placed my clothes where we kept dirty clothes for laundry later I knelt down to the God, The God I knew Lord Jesus Christ and asked him to forgive me, to have succumbed to the demands of these forces of evil, I acknowledged before God the only sacrifice I know for humanity is his sacrificial lamb Lord Jesus Christ, I felt the Presence of the Holy Spirit which assured me God have heard my prayer, I was a confused person, I didn't know what to do next, I consoled myself and forgave them hoping they will learn something new.

I tried to engage Mungiki in political ideas that I thought would yield to better interaction with the wider community but Mungiki leadership had their own vision and goals, they tried to engage Democratic party for party politics and after their usual mode of operation achieved their intention, Ndura Waruinge took Money from Hon Chris Murungaru former Internal security minister and Hon Matu Wamae former M.P Mathira, an arrangement that was to buy mobile phones for Mungiki members, he divided the loot with Maina Njenga.

Maina Njenga felt he is the anointed Kikuyu Caliph of the "Kirinyaga kingdom", ethnic caliphate. He therefore made a pretense to support somebody but actually he had his own goals.

My nature couldn't be hidden for long, I was unable to contain hypocrisy and assume all is well, a trend that was seen as rebellion and a verdict had been reached without my knowledge. Questioning Mungiki leaders exposing their evil was death.

Democratic party, the party that somehow was seen as better placed to wrestle power from the ruling party KANU had sought for Mungiki support and Ndura Waruinge took me to meet Hon Chris Murungaru, Matu Wamae and Dr. Gikonyo in a secret arranged meeting in Dr. Gikonyo office at Nairobi hospital. These politicians agreed to finance a project to arm Mungiki with mobile phones to ease communication among them. My pretense of appearing to be one of them was not meant to go far, it is difficult to make a sheep behave like a goat and briefly I had learned this is a death trap, where every perceived enemy is killed.

I reported Mungiki activities to then Buru Buru Police Station [O.C.S] but to my amazement he did not enquire more and make arrest, he told me he is aware of all those allegations', I therefore sought to report these Mungiki activities to the National security intelligence service and with a help of a close relative from my in laws, I met the external Director of National Security Service Mr. Petkay Miriti who wrote a wide detailed account on Mungiki activities.

In the few weeks that followed I was a marked man for elimination and I also learned from a close confidant working in Buru Buru Police station that my house had a search warrant, I was afraid why was the government targeting me as a whistle blower by questioning Mungiki leadership and exposing their evil among themselves, could it be they want me silenced because I might be a voice exposing a partnership that was in a pipeline between the government and Mungiki militias perceived by international community as criminals?, I pondered.

A hired assassin a Mr. Cliff Ruai Karume who was later killed by Mungiki came and spilled the beans to me, he told me he has been hired to kill me but his conscious had questioned." why should I be killed"? I immediately knew my life was in danger and having observed the Police response after I had reported Mungiki activities to them, I got my passport ready, asked Cliff "if he could accompany me for a visit to Tanzania at my cost," I also engaged another Mungiki leader D.O, Kamau Mwathi. who agreed to accompany us for that visit to Tanzania?

I wrote several letters to media houses, trying to expose Mungiki activities and reported my plight to Kenya Embassy in Tanzania. A Kenya Diplomat by the name of Bundotich helped me pass a complain to the Kenya government by a letter to the President Moi telling him I was actually supporting the idea for the youth to partner with Uhuru Kenyatta.

President Moi had already shown deep interest in endorsing Uhuru Kenyatta as his successor and I reasoned my support of Uhuru Kenyatta would be well received by President Moi and reverse ill-advised decision that may have construed me as an enemy, my guess was right after some days I received a call through the Kenya embassy in Dar es Salaam from the Director External Intelligent National security service Mr. Petkay Miriti.

I was called back home by Petkay Miriti Director external Intelligent National Security Service who assured me of my safety and we meet several times in Boulevard hotel and Norfolk hotel Nairobi and in one of this meetings he told me," as we are speaking now, Mungiki leaders had already seen the President and there is little you can do or stop their activities all," 'what had been agreed on, the only suggestion that exist is to register a political party to be financed by National Intelligence service, bring Mungiki trusted leaders on board as well as other youths from different communities and form a coalition to work with KANU".I coiled myself and realized these forces are unstoppable and uncertainty lied ahead.

I was given some money and told to make enquires on the available names for party registration at the registrar of societies at Attorney general's chambers.

 Ndura Waruinge mocked me and asked me where else can I report them now they are with the government, for fear of life and action by angry Mungiki adherents because of a strife that was growing within Mungiki as a result of my complain about the assassination plot by Ndura Waruinge who had sent the hired assassin Cliff Ruai Karume, a hearing of my case was scheduled by Mungiki oath administrators but I resolved not to attend the case. I reasoned if the case was established and Ndura Waruinge found guilty, I wasn't ready for the consequences he would had faced, I decided to forgave him rather than face a life torment of a verdict by Mungiki oath administrators.

I was later tracked in the offices of Sisi Kwa Sisi political party and to my surprise, an oath den had been set already in one of their offices and for a second time, I found myself facing an oath administrator for a step two of a Mungiki oath with a code "Kilima" you answer "Ira" ,or "Ira," you answer "Kilima" ,I tried to fool them that I have passed this stage after I had learned a third stage code, "freedom -2000", "Uhuru -2000", from my friend Cliff but I didn't know which is second or third. I therefore had to again succumb to the demands of these evil forces. I obliged and with few beatings this second time, I took the oath.

The swearing in this second stage of a Mungiki recruit was directed to obey Mungiki leadership without question but to me this was my last encounter with an oath administrator.

I had learned a lesson, tricks and maneuvers that traps potential oath victims and I had become wise. Several traps to lure me to oath dens were laid, but none succeeded and at one time they forcefully attempted to kidnap me in broad daylight in Ikinu market Kiambu after I had advanced my war with Mungiki by producing videos that exposed and condemned their activities.

Before the Kidnap event in Ikinu- Kiambu, I had arrived in a decision that it was practically impossible for me to survive in the midst of these evil forces and thought of relocating to a different location since they had already known where lived, my worries were also built on the idea from the National security service which I wasn't ready for.

A good Samaritan had hinted to me that working with National intelligent security Service might ultimately end up in elimination. I wasn't ready to travel in a path of unknown obstacles. I fled the country again and landed in Dar es Salaam Tanzania.

My life had been shaken by forces beyond me and in a such situation, only another force a mightier power can help, I therefore sought divine help and I prayed asking God to let me die, help me understand the path I'm travelling or simply let me agree with evil and never judge me for my actions. God answers prayer.

A story had appeared in a front page of a local daily The Guardian, a leading Tanzania Newspaper, a report I had written earlier to The United Nations after I had learned that powerful personalities within the government were allowing DRC Congo rebels use Kenya as a transit point for the ill-gotten wealth that was financing anti-governments forces in The DRC Congo,

The report was commended by DRC ambassador to Tanzania by then Ambassador Theodore Mugalu who later became known to me as a staunch Christian believer and he helped me understand how these forces of evil that I had running from do operate.

He was God sent help and after brief stay in Dar es Salaam, I gathered courage and by faith believing God as my protector, I was ready to return to Kenya and face these evil forces.

 At Namanga immigration Tanzania border control point, my passport was scrutinized and scrutinized again, Kenya government had secretly tracked me for reasons unknown to me and asked their counterparts the Tanzanian government for assistance, I was arrested and handed over to the Kenyan immigration officials, reasons not given.

The following morning, I was taken to Nyayo house Nairobi immigration department where I underwent a series of interviews and later locked up in kileleshwa police station, after two days in the police cells, one interview after another, the order came from above and I was set free but my passport was confiscated.

The next few months towards 2002 general elections I was in low profile, I refused to join the Uhuru Kenyatta/Mungiki partnership even after I was seduced with money and position, I had learned a lesson.

CHAPTER FOUR:

UHURU KENYATTA / MUNGIKI CONNECTION.

The opposition didn't capture the political power from the incumbent President Moi in 1992 nor did they capture it 1997 and though in both election tribal clashes were experienced, but it is worthy to note for the purpose of tracing the evil seed, Mungiki in 1997 didn't distribute its propaganda leaflets in Rift valley. Tribal clashes were not experienced in Rift valley, only in Mombasa. Mungiki actually did nothing to defend the community from these clashes, in 1992 as earlier said, it was in its formation and its most activity was initiating new recruits or mobilizing support and due to its nature of ideology it wasn't received very well across board in many Kikuyu homes, even the few who somehow felt the brunt of the violence in 1992 tribal violence were not ready for this new ideology that seemed strange to the new generation.

Mungiki marshalled its strength when it got State support after meeting with President Moi and launching a political unity of supporting Uhuru Kenyatta Presidential ambition, it became a wild dog on the loose and confrontational clashes emerged as the one witnessed in Kariobangi Nairobi March 2002 after some of their members were attacked by some members from the Luo community, they had to perform a show of might and prove to the community that, they were ready for engagement to defend their interests.

After establishing its roots and branding itself as the Kikuyu Militia army and with the support of political personality with blessing of Mau Mau, Mungiki was ready to establish its political recognition as an entity of the kikuyu community ready to establish an ethnic caliphate.

President Daniel Moi, who was now grooming Uhuru Kenyatta to take the Political leadership was a darling of the Mungiki, he didn't take any serious measure to crash Mungiki, in fact he never showed any out of the ordinary interest to fully understand the goals of Mungiki either he knew they didn't pose any serious threat to his rule or he had the hidden card, to give them Uhuru Kenyatta, a Kikuyu, one their own."

"We meet President Moi for a second time through the help of Hon Njenga Karume and the former Kenya power Managing Director Julius Gichuru as David narrates, and we learned that President Moi had no problem with   our activities of mobilizing our community and he personally told us in a later meeting his intentions were to hand over power to Hon Uhuru Kenyatta, he was friendly and showed a sense of unity and due to his approach we had fully respect to President Moi, our mission gave birth to another a meeting in kabarak Nakuru, where we met Hon Uhuru Kenyatta, 'former Thika KANU chairman' Paul Hato and we all agreed to mobilize the community in support of Uhuru Kenyatta" These meeting took place sometimes in 2001.

"We were told that we would also be supported if we wanted to vie Parliamentary seats, councilors seats and we would form the next government with Hon Uhuru Kenyatta"." We were given money to continue with our mobilization and guaranteed government support". David continues.

"We therefore continued with oath taking rituals and came up a new oath code which was to support Uhuru Kenyatta and also help us get support from the community, the secret code that we came with was" Uhuru-

2000", meaning came the year 2002, Uhuru would be the President and we would get freedom, in English the code was" freedom-2000".

Secret codes are used to identify those that have taken oath, whenever one takes oath, a code to prove one has taken the oath is passed to the new recruits and if you are asked the code, there is an expected answer proving that you have passed that stage of the oath, Mungiki new recruit code was "Nyaga" then you answer "Ruoya", or "Ruoya then you answer "Nyaga" that is the first stage of a fresh recruit."

"Hon Uhuru Kenyatta contributed very generously to this course with car donation, money and we met several times joking as comrades, and Uhuru would refer me David as "baba" in Kikuyu meaning father, he was quite happy with our support but complained very much about our gears, the paraphernalia we carried, tobacco sniffing, sticks, machetes and our aggressiveness which was perceived to be outdated and we were advised to change, but Maina Njenga our spiritual leader wanted us to remain as we were with our own branding and identity, he didn't want us to change".

"Uhuru Kenyatta was not happy and after a meeting in his office in chancellery building, he advised me and my cousin Joe

Waiganjo.to take some steps and make a coup in Mungiki by eliminating Maina Njenga and Ndura Waruinge and he promised to fund that coup and elimination, a task we were not very ready to undertake"." This created a gap that made Uhuru doubt our friendship and capabilities".

Uhuru Kenyatta didn't want that Mungiki image but wanted to ride on their gained efforts and like his father, the first president of Kenya Jomo Kenyatta, who also distanced himself from Mau Mau but was a Mau Mau according to Mau Mau oath administrator Kimamo Wanjohi, he Kenyatta rode on Mau Mau gains used their ignorance and became the president of Kenya, likewise Uhuru wanted to follow the same steps

"Uhuru Kenyatta close friend Hon David Murathe had advised him that, we were very dangerous people, David continues, 'and 'we were capable of giving him an oath in his own car and he should be very careful when dealing with us', this we learned after Uhuru Kenyatta convened a meeting with us Mungiki leaders in Quality hotel in Hurlingham were he narrated to us what Hon Murathe had told him, but being brave enough he told us he would choose whom to believe, we or Hon Murathe".

In Quality hotel meeting David continues," we were many Mungiki leaders 12 of us in all,

I David Wagacha, Maina Njenga, Ndura Waruinge, Charles Ndungu, George Wagacha, Joe waiganjo, Kimani Ruo and many other Mungiki leaders".

"Maina Njenga had advised us not to give Uhuru Kenyatta the oath and the likes of Hon Njenga Karume, we were therefore not ready to decoy or trap Uhuru Kenyatta for the oath taking but somehow he believed Hon David Murathe and started distancing himself".

"The kikuyu community was very much divided on whom exactly to support in 2002 general election, KANU which we supported lost miserably to NARC party headed by Mwai Kibaki who became the 3rd Kenya president and we were also denied KANU nomination after we became adamant to the change that Uhuru Kenyatta wanted. Word had gone round that our status which was seen outdated would be counterproductive and create a bad image to the ruling party, we were therefore denied party nomination".

"We therefore met Hon Uhuru Kenyatta through President Moi support and our own initiative to support him in his 2002 Presidential ambition, and he was truly friendly and a comrade who treated us as equals, he supported us with Money and logistics, not once but several times, he never liked our Mungiki brand image of tobacco sniffing, machetes, dreadlocks, Mungiki flags and such, he was willing to work with us but our spiritual leader Maina Njenga was not ready for that change and the only hard word that was a point to ponder as David narrates was "why can't you eliminate Maina Njenga and Ndura Waruinge for the change I want"," I'm ready to finance the cost involved", honestly were not ready for that. why?' We never thought of Mungiki without Maina Njenga,' and our ambitions at that time were very limited within us, as a group".

"Maina Njenga was not ready to surrender his efforts of forming Mungiki and surrender his authority to Uhuru Kenyatta by agreeing with his plans and change, he perceived himself also a leader of the ethnic caliphate - Kikuyu Kirinyaga kingdom, he was a "mumbui" just like Uhuru and within Mungiki circles, it was known that their struggle is not about Kenya but ethnic leadership, which they saw it with Maina Njenga".

CHAPTER   FIVE.

MWAI KIBAKI 2002 VICTORY AND THE CRACKDOWN.

Mwai kibaki won the election and became the president of Kenya in 2002 with a landslide victory and Uhuru Kenyatta became the leader of the opposition. Kikuyu mainstream community was supporting Mwai Kibaki and after Kibaki had formed the government, he called Mungiki to surrender through his Minister of internal security Chris Murungaru, [in the same line of thought as what had happened in 1963], when the first president Jomo Kenyatta had taken the Mantle of political leadership, he demanded and called the other Mau Mau to surrender and those that didn't surrender like General Baimungi from Meru were killed and others fled the country.

Ndura Waruinge who was by then the National Mungiki coordinator surrendered, other defectors who defected and openly started exposing Mungiki activities were the gospel music artists from River rd. Nairobi.

Maina Njenga leading other Mungiki members declared a clandestine economic empowerment program that touched transport industry and criminal activities, they became adamant to support the Kibaki government. Violence erupted in Nakuru after Mungiki members were attacked and Mungiki revenged with massacres and Kibaki stretched his muscles to crash them. They were disappointed, they had never thought Mwai Kibaki would be the president. A mystery cloud hanged ahead, Maina Njenga ambition of being a Kikuyu caliph in waiting and a power broker in Uhuru Kenya government had dwindled.

Mungiki had fully anticipated that Uhuru would have won the General election, their code Uhuru-2000 turned to a wide dream, Maina was believed to be a prophet and when the promised freedom was not realized some Mungiki doubted his prophecies and openly challenged his call as a prophet

Maina Njenga feared Mungiki might turn against him and thought to redirect the organization to Christianity so that he can change their faith, many disagreed and called themselves "Kiama kia mutitu", meaning they belong to forest or are forest fighters.

The Narc government had vowed to crash Mungiki and had been miss-informed about a scenario where Mungiki had been given old Military land lovers by President Moi and the internal security Minister Hon Chris

Murungaru said, "Mungiki was Militarily preparing to challenge the government and the government would face them militarily".

I inquired from my cousins about those land lovers and called the Internal Security Minister Chris Murungaru to clarify to him that the land rovers were actually gifts from the 'former President during campaigns,' and Mungiki had no military capacity to the challenge the government. An official from the ministry later called and asked me to write a proposal on how we can rehabilitate Mungiki adherents.

I wrote a report that created a NARC government policy to deal with Mungiki and other idle youths, absorbing some in National youth service, enrolling some in village polytechnics and starting a radio program in a local Kikuyu vernacular station whose aim was to mentally reverse their believe in the rituals and oaths they had taken.

I was not invited in the execution these proposals, the government took my idea and tried to rehabilitate Mungiki as per the proposal, it never worked, they tried to an extend of establishing the youth empowerment program, but Mungiki remained a challenge to the authorities because the main player Maina Njenga was still active poisoning their minds.

I started my own program to spiritually reverse their believes in the Kikuyu rituals by preaching to them Christianity and a group that had emerged calling itself "Kiama kia Mutitu" posed a danger to few who were responding to this program and Maina Njenga fearing that group, he completely sabotaged my initiative of rehabilitation by creating fear among the respondents, but a seed had been planted among the gospel artists who defected from Mungiki.

A group of gospel musician who had taken this Kikuyu oath, among them the famous Kikuyu artist Muigai wa Njoroge, "Njohorai minyororo," comedian "Nyengese", the late Macharia wa Karanja [Kamucumari] kumomora to Uritu. and several other artists who were performing in downtown River rd. near OTC Nairobi. They openly challenged Mungiki authority through song and street preaching and as result war was declared on them. Over 14 in number including a hired assassin who had been hired by Ndura Waruinge to kill me Cliff Karume were killed. I escaped this massacre by the mercies of God, I had to relocate my residence to a hotel. [Follow this link 14 Mungiki defectors Killed].

Kibaki administration with the help of Mungiki defectors targeted Maina Njenga and other Mungiki leaders who were arrested and charged with the death of defectors, a case that had to be compromised between Mungiki and defectors after witnesses were threatened and the killing of defectors continued, the prosecution lost the case and Maina Njenga and other Mungiki leaders were released.

Mungiki proved to the authorities it's a force to reckon with and by crook and hook they proved they are not disintegrating anytime soon, as it is proven through the following subsequent events.

The Kenya constitution referendum of 2005 awakened a dialogue between Mungiki and the government, Kibaki-NARC party had serious problems after they failed to honor the memorandum of understanding he had with his coalition partners and his support had dwindled. He therefore tried to lure Mungiki to support the government but majority of the Mungiki went the side of Uhuru Kenyatta to the "NO" team or orange symbol though they had pocketed a lot of money given to them by Kibaki administration to lure them, this didn't sink well with kibaki administration and immediately after the humiliating defeat in the referendum, he restarted a campaign that had seemed forgotten, Mungiki crackdown as Joe Waiganjo, the Mungiki spokesman pointed out.

Mathare Valley in Nairobi bore the brunt of the crackdown effects that Kibaki administration demonstrated in 2006 and early 2007 crackdown. In one such incident, in a single day 35 people perceived to be Mungiki members were killed, women raped and in a span of hours Mathare slums looked like a war zone, this was after they had ambushed some police officers on patrol and shot them.

Kibaki administration through his internal security minister by then Hon John Michuki had earlier convened a meeting of all Kikuyu M. Ps and declared a war on Mungiki, a kitty had been launched as a show of support and reward to the police officers who were to be tasked with the Job of promoting "Mungiki to glory" a term that was used by this police killing squad-code named "KweKwe", the code meant killing them. This information was relied to Mungiki through close confidants of Mungiki like Hon John Mututho 'former M.P Naivasha', Hon Guyai 'former M.P Kikuyu' and Hon Njenga Karume 'former cabinet minister defense, 'every M.P was asked to donate one million Kenya shillings as a sign of support to the task of cracking down Mungiki and show solidarity to the policy of Kibaki regime of extra-Judicial execution.

Many youths were killed official documented figures stood at over 600 youths killed through extrajudicial execution and one such report documented was by Kenya National Human right commission report. Cry of Blood' Report on Extrajudicial Killings. Musau Ndunda a secretary with Release Political prisoners pressure group fled the country as well as others like Kamanda Mucheke of Kenya human rights commission, other reports from the United Nations special Rapporteur Philip Alston also condemned these widespread atrocities committed by the government.

Oscar kingara, of Oscar foundation a human rights lawyer was also killed in cold blood along with his colleague near Nairobi university. He had also documented this extra-judicial execution by Kibaki administration which will go down in history as a worst form of brutality that was done in a criminal like execution by a legitimate elected government, it was a worst form of approach to tame these youths, dismembered body parts were thrown in many parts of the country and some youths disappeared without trace, a cry that was felt all over central Kenya, young men missing, this scenario was worse resembled the same kind of torture that was rendered to Mau Mau by the British during the Mau Mau war.

[Ref Imperial Reckoning - Caroline Elkins - Macmillan].

Jomo Kenyatta also had called the surrender of the Mau Mau and he dealt ruthlessly and firmly with those that refused to surrender. It is believed that Maina Njenga partnered with the government to eliminate those that he perceived as his enemies because his life was not in a serious threat even though he was the leader of Mungiki, he somehow convinced the government that, though he supported the government during referendum some Mungiki elements were going against his leadership and were anti-government and should be eliminated, and one such incident is how Kimani Ruo who was the Rift Valley Mungiki coordinator died who though they had been arrested together, Kimani Ruo disappeared and Maina life was spared, a story told by one of the police officer Bernard Kiriinya. [Ref KNCHR Releases Testimony of Late Bernard Kiriinya on ...] The report to Kenya human rights commission was his confession how him and other police officers were mobilized to set a killing squad code named kweKwe and finally how they lured Kimani Ruo to his death, he also details how other Mungiki members were killed. These orders points to a fact that there were those that were marked for death. Bernard

Kiriinya was not spared either after that disclosure, he was shot in Westland Nairobi.

I also took an initiative to produce an audio visual "Mungiki Mystery documentary, documenting these crimes done by the government, part one of this documentary exposed this evil committed by a legitimate government in a criminal like execution and part two exposing Mungiki oath activities.

The part two of this documentary was a bitter seed for Mungiki to swallow and my head was demanded through unceasing phone calls but God preserved me, they were unable to reach me. That exposure and fear sent a strong message to Mungiki and they started having doubts on their faith and Maina Njenga took the advantage of this opportunity to literally tell Mungiki they should be prepared for change. Maina Njenga was in prison charged with massacre in Kirinyaga district where 29 people were killed.

Leadership is a noble call and it is an office of honor and respect. Political leaders are called to protect the lives of all poor, rich, criminals and every subject under their jurisdiction by the rule of law that made them leaders, when they fail to do so, they subject the entire population into a lawlessness society, in innocence, one questions their decisions and though

Mungiki were real devils, but do governments turns and acts like criminals to prove a point, what's the purpose of laws and parliament?

Tribal Militias are barbaric and their ideologies and forceful support of a cause that deny individual freedom of choice is ungodly, primitive and unacceptable in a civilized world, Mungiki actions of beheading their victims, dismembered of victim's body parts or forceful oath administration is the most soul tormenting evil that one can do to a fellow human being and that can only be likened with what ISIS is doing in the middle east or their counterparts Al-Shabaab in Somalia.

At one time of Mungiki transformation and mutations, they became Muslims and attended madras in Kwale and Kikambala Mombasa, Maina Njenga became Mohamed, David Wagacha-Hassan, Ndura Waruinge-Ibrahim and Charles Ndungu Wagacha-Ramadhan. Muslim scholars who received them and tried to analyze the nature of spirit in Maina Njenga referred it as "Jinni" Arabic -meaning demon. Mungiki formation and growth has a spiritual significant worth noting for scholars researching spiritual radicalism and tracing certain spiritual elements of prophecy and seed.

This can unlock at great length the nature of spirits awakening, and create awareness. Our human positioning in clans, tribes, race, nations and religion can be manipulated through prophecy to fulfill certain evil goals

Mungiki massacres, beheadings, in Nakuru, Kariobangi, Kirinyaga and several parts of Kiambu, Muranga and Nyeri as was witnessed was truly a concern and any authority would have proved its legitimacy by establishing order, rule of law and bringing to book these evil doers, who happened to be murderers, arsonists, kidnappers and a civilized plan within the established laws would have ended and got rid of this kind of evil.

Maina Njenga belongs to jail and a court process with a total commitment to the protection of witnesses would have helped solve the mystery behind Mungiki ideology but when a government choose other criminal methods to get rid of this kind of evil and partnering with the same evil to achieve individual selfish goals, one wonders, what lessons are they teaching the future generation? where are we as a society? Politics based on tribal numbers, tribal coalition, tribal interests and goals should be a thing of the past, we live as individuals protected by the rule of law and it is a God given right of self will to determine who to vote for or support and until we came to that realization, our knowledge of God, moral standing and intellect remain imprisoned by mental concepts of slavery that positions and poisons our minds and hearts as custodians of clans interests, tribes, race, color and religion. When these terms define us were no better than savages.

CHAPTER   SIX:

THE   2007/8   GENERAL ELECTION   AND   THE   POST ELECTION VIOLENCE.
THE CONSPIRACY.

General elections should not be a mark that controls and defines who we are, but it should be a process that civilized people determines their leaders. The process should always be received accepted and taken as just another day, a democratic process where free people are able to decide their leaders. Integrity, visionary and basic moral values should be what determines the candidature of these leaders, constitution should not be words just written in books only known for to the judges and lawyers but a way of life that determines and defines a society.

Uphold to rule of law positions a Nation and character is shaped that demands respect, sovereignty and independency. Without character of the rule of law any other power somewhere can challenge the sovereignty and independence that determines and define that society. [Ref Rome Statute]

Kibaki administration was scared that they could lose the 2007/8 general election and in their individual selfish interest to remain in power, or "selfish community interests", on the eventuality of the power shifting base to another community, they considered many options irrespective of integrity, morality and character that defines a person and evil was better than hope, vomit was better than sacrifice, their ego and pride won't allow a defeat or an unknown eventuality. That fear planned, cooked and dished all pain that brought up 2007/8 general election violence and all events that followed.

Unknown skeptical fear of leadership from other tribe than a Kikuyu enslaves many Kikuyus and creates mistrust across board among major tribes of Kenya, a scenario that ought to change if Kenyans as individuals are willing to free themselves from this mental slavery that has developed as a faith, as a religion, as an ideology and many serves evil, tagged as community interests, though by age these tribal leaders should be teachers, but they have returned to their vomit and worst of it they are blind to reality.

When the 2007 general election approached PNU,' [Party of national unity] think tank with Kibaki being the driver invited Mungiki to State house, a meeting that they have repeatedly sworn that it never took place but repeating a lie don't change a fact, for truth has roots and is backed by its foundation, proving by producing a manifest of the youths that went to State House in November 26th 2007,puts a serious investigator a feet forward for by having that manifest alone, that proves actually a meeting took place, and the manifest itself has names of those that we have insisted that were Mungiki representatives that visited state house, that is the truth that cannot be annulled no matter how disputed. Various groups were invited to state house on this day of November 26. 2007 and each group had their own agenda.

 Among the youths, who of course didn't go with the name Mungiki were Mungiki representative Godwin Kamau Wangoe, Maina Kangethe" Diambo, Wagikura to name a few. Godwin Kamau Wangoe had with him a document that was the basis of the meeting to reconcile Mungiki and the government, a report that he had been instructed to write by Geoffrey Machira, the link man referred in PNU circles as Mr. Network and Ambassador Francis Muthaura. This report was to be acted on by the government and it required Kibaki blessings.

Wangoe read the document and presented it to the president. The contents were grievances and were in very simple words stop the harassment of the Kikuyu youths in Central province, stop extra-judicial execution, release Maina Njenga [who by then was in prison] and we Mungiki will support you in 2007 general election. Nothing else had meaning beyond those words any other words were just protocol and formalities.

That was the memorandum of grievances presented to the President of Kenya Mwai Kibaki in 26th November 2007 by Godwin Kamau Wangoe a Mungiki representative contacted through Geoffrey Machira a music producer in downtown River Road Nairobi and the Secretary to the Cabinet Francis Muthaura who aided the Nairobi State house visit.

 Kibaki administration came with a program, a policy to integrate Mungiki back as partners and 'probably be standby Kikuyu Militia to be used if so required,' a Militia to defend an ethnic caliphate that Kibaki had assumed leadership [These is proven by various other meetings that Mungiki leaders attended in Zambezi motel Muguga, Brackenhurst Tigoni and etc.]. The State House meeting gave birth to other various meeting and open air crusades that saw

Mungiki permitted to use their cleansing ritual ceremonies and such open air meetings were held in Uhuru Park Nairobi and Thika Stadium under the Chairmanship of Rev Samuel Murigu the former east Africa moderator of the PCEA church.

Rev Samuel Murigu of PCEA church and other church ministers hosted Mungiki in various, places i.e. Brackenhurst Tigoni, Uhuru Park Nairobi and Thika Stadium, I attended several of these meetings after getting an invitation to document these events, I was in a process of gathering information for my audio visual documentary Mungiki Mystery and I took this golden chance to document what was happening, Rev Murigu clearly informed Mungiki that the Kikuyu Caliphate "Nyumba ya Mumbi "government was not ready to relinquish power and they needed support of Mungiki.

In these meetings several scenarios were discussed that suggested an already determined position in regard to the general election that was take place in few weeks' time, a determined decision had been arrived that "Nyumba ya Mumbi" would protect its ethnic acquired leadership, it was a conspiracy that saw Mungiki free and dining with the same people that had earlier campaigned to eliminate them. Why does one support an army that cannot be contained when there is no war? tribal militias are like any conventional army, and they need rehabilitation after ceasefire and by saying that I'm not approving a tribal militia but pointing to some irresponsible actions.

The Kikuyu community had been duped and supported Mungiki, an army, they could not contain due to power wrangles as who heads the ethnic kingdom, political intellectuals saw themselves as automatic bonafide leaders of this traditional militias created by rituals, whereas Mungiki members had learned a lesson through history, they were not ready to blindly follow the demands and direction of this political elites.

Maina Njenga had all the cards that control and direct Mungiki, prophecy and "ndumeriri" inspired dreams or messages. The political elites had thought Kikuyu church leaders had a better chance to negotiate this deal but were taken for a ride, Maina Njenga loves money and he had a commodity to sell," ni kaogi" a term meaning you need to be wise, such a term was a driving factor in such a dialogue. The same mode of operation could have been used in triggering the tribal clashes.

Mungiki was free again protected and supported by the government, the extra-judicial execution briefly stopped and Mungiki launched a major campaign to recruit more followers through oath administration, they would be arrested but a phone call to Geoffrey Machira, who would then call Francis Muthaura would immediately solve the problem and Mungiki released.

One such incident happened in Muranga and Kawangware in Nairobi. In Muranga they had gathered for a meeting to deliberate these issues they were riding on, supporting the government and in Kawangware, they were arrested in actual oath administration process but a phone call away solved the problem, these incidents are perfects leads that positions, Francis Muthaura, Mwai Kibaki, internal security Minister by then John Michuki into corroboration with Mungiki that cemented their relationship prior to 2007/8 general election.

State house provided money, Mungiki was financed to mobilize the youth and key Mungiki trustees whose hands was used as confidants of Maina Njenga were Kangethe Maina "Diambo" and Godwin Kamau Wangoe. Millions of Kenya shillings were paid to Maina Njenga, Geoffrey Machira being the link man.

Mungiki music artists also played a major role to mobilize the Mungiki across Central

Kenya and Rift valley provinces to awaken the Mungiki spirit, 'ethnic- Kingdom' and integrate them back to the community having suffered the crackdown and extra-judicial execution. Maina Njenga was promised release and Kikuyu militia spirit was alive.

Kikuyu leaders in the government had conspired and brought Mungiki on board, the then President Mwai Kibaki, Cabinet Minister John Michuki, secretary to the Cabinet Francis Muthaura and other Kikuyu personalities turned their back and forgot their official government image that carries the respect of their office, they changed their intellectual understanding and smeared their character with vomit by engaging in the same evil that they had tried to contain.

Through fear and ego, selfish driven unknown community skeptical reasoning, they completely destroyed their persona and they preferred gloom, rather light. One question this kind of character, how far can this mental slavery imprison one soul? Person's seen as teachers, elders, role models worth of admiration, lied low to the level Kikuyu villagers living in 16 century.

Mau Mau/Mungiki conspiracy of recognition and blessing through outdated Kikuyu rituals that completely destroys individual rights and liberty to free will and choice was now officially recognized backed by legitimate government of intellectuals, if this kind of character is not hellish, one wonder what is evil, for evil can be forgiven in the heart of an illiterate soul but when practiced by a literate well informed person, that can only explain one thing, such a soul is already imprisoned in hell a bondage that require an extra insight probably beyond the five senses.

Church leaders like the one mentioned, Rev Samuel Murigu of PCEA church fell also into that trap not only him but many others as well, though freedom and liberation comes from the Bible the Word of God, they discarded that and their selfish hearts overcame their reasoning and blinded their faith and instead of being teachers, they became tombs haunted by Kikuyu tribal spirits,

During 2007/8 general election Uhuru Kenyatta whose party was KANU had opted to support PNU and he therefore had no direct special interest as an individual to get support from Mungiki and the issue here was not an Uhuru Kenyatta issue, though he was a Kikuyu leader, the connection link between Mungiki and PNU was Francis Muthaura through Geoffrey Machira, the Music producer.

Through the National intelligence service, Kibaki administration had learned and realized that the Kalenjin tribe had planned to evict the Kikuyus from Rift valley whether ODM won or not and they feared the eventuality of a worse scenario, the government could not have used its machinery to counter the Kalenjin militias probably they reasoned.

Tribal politics fuels such unknown eventualities but the answer doesn't lie in evil encountering evil but in truth. Though a real threat was over the horizon, Kibaki should have shown maturity of a leader by sending clear signals as soon as he ascended to power that tribal politics is a game played by savages, primitive barbarians. He should have honored a fact that his presidency was in fact not a game of tribal card.

Kibaki administration under the command of John Michuki Minister internal security, his lieutenants, Francis Kimemia, Francis Muthaura felt that Mungiki was needed to counter the Kalenjin Militias. This is evident by what Mungiki alleged to have transpired later.

The Kalenjin tribesmen had prepared for kikuyu eviction long before election, an almost a repetitive occurrence that would normally occur during every general election and after the election, as it was widely rumored that ODM had won and denied victory, the Kalenjin warriors started their long perceived plans the eviction of the Kikuyus, which was well planned coordinated and executed. WHO PLANTED THIS SEED?

 A' former workmate in Beta Healthcare Int' who lived near Yamubi village Eldoret called Serem told me about the planned eviction and attacks before they could be executed, proving a well-conceived and coordinated idea.

Kikuyus from Central province knows very little of what exactly happened in Rift Valley especially Molo area, Eldoret and Turbo areas, Kikuyus in large numbers suffered a lot, they were evicted in thousands, houses burnt, and many killed by arrows, spears and machetes.

Kiambaa church burning where women and children were burnt alive hit the headlines and moved other Kikuyus to action, by demonstrating in Nairobi and demanding action from the government, one such demonstration was led by 'former Mungiki National coordinator 'Ndura Waruinge. WHY WARUINGE? A former Mungiki national coordinator.

Several meetings took place in Nairobi, different professional gathered in various hotels, groups across board from as far as Eldoret held meetings in various hotels to deliberate what to do and what kind of support they could render to their fellow tribesmen in Rift valley, one such meeting we attended was on at Jacaranda Hotel Westland Nairobi, a Hotel owned by Hon Njenga Karume, 'former Minister of defense'.

In this hotel, Njenga Karume had allowed a group led by 'former Molo M.P' Njenga Mungai and Molo residents to converge here to deliberate issues and help and the way forward, several issues were discussed among them, what kind of support the government can give, it was agreed that the community need funds, weapons, logistical support and young men to counter these attacks, I ,David Waithaka Wagacha and Joe Waiganjo,[the Mungiki spokesman by then] was in this meeting and we were clearly told the president and the government was behind us as David narrates ,"they fully supported the agenda of the meeting".

"The Kikuyu community with a full backing of the government, Mwai kibaki the President of Kenya, Kikuyu leaders and church leaders, businessmen and legislators mobilized resources from every quarter, guns were bought from as far as Laikipia".

I personally received updates from the people who were known to us from Kimuri Village and were victims of these atrocities especially in the Kiambaa Church burning, Kikuyus especially in these areas never fought back many fled and others were killed. The remaining Kikuyu population that had not fled in 1992 tribal violence had no option but to flee, many suffered loss and to date though the government talks of IDP resettlement, many who never went to these IDP camps live today with losses suffered from these clashes.

David continues to state that "Kibaki administration through the use of administration police moved in to counter these attacks and Kinuthia Mbugua A.P commandant, Francis Kimemia, Hon John Michuki and other Kikuyu government officials drew a plan to involve Mungiki and to counter these atrocities, but Mungiki wasn't ready", Majority of Mungiki though having been lured to support PNU had outwitted them and were busy during these clashes recruiting more followers rather fighting back in fact many had opted to support ODM and were happy that a prophecy that had made them look like outcasts was unfolding.

"Ndura Waruinge reached out and sort Mungiki help, he called former Mungiki acting Chairman by then Charles Ndungu Wagacha to a meeting in Cargen House under the chair of Michuki wife Watiri and a personal assistant to Hon John Michuki Mr. Mwaura. In this meeting, Waruinge, Charles Ndungu, Naftali Irungu, Kangethe Maina "Diambo" Timothy Mburu, "Wagatira", Maina Waithaka," guka", and Njoroge "Wagichere", were instructed what to do as David narrates.

"Francis Kimemia and Kinuthia Mbugua drew a plan to retaliate the Kalenjin attacks and areas were marked up for these retaliatory attacks, being Dandora Kibera, Kawangware and Naivasha".

"Kinuthia Mbugua provided guns and uniforms, through Francis kimemia who was used to distribute the uniforms and guns", kimemia called me personally David continues," and told me to go to state House Nakuru to collect uniforms and guns, he had called my brother Charles Ndungu Wagacha earlier who had given him my phone number, to pick money, uniforms and guns in John Michuki wife Watiri office at Cargen house Nairobi", "Kibaki administration used the administration police vehicles through the command of Kinuthia Mbugua". " These uniforms and guns came from administration police training in Embakasi".

"The Mungiki leaders who were in that meeting a Cargen house had represented various locations where these uniforms and guns were to be used, Maina Waithaka" guka" was a coordinator of Kibera, Njoroge "Wagichere "was the Dandora representative and though some may have used them or mobilized their areas to stage attacks, the wider Mungiki fraternity were not directly in these attacks and after realizing that Mungiki was not automatically supporting the government idea, a new recruitment exercise, oath administration was started through Ndura Waruinge in a forest near Naivasha, idle Kikuyu youths were picked up in kayole area, Naivasha, Kinangop area, Engineer and taken to a forest near Naivasha where they were given a Mungiki oath and this is the group that was used for retaliatory attacks in Naivasha but this plan was arranged and hatched in Naivasha at Belle Inn hotel under the command of Ndura Waruinge, 'former Naivasha M.P Jane kihara, 'former Mayor of Naivasha', a local councilor and some Mungiki members in Naivasha, "as David states.

I had also gathered some information from other sources in Kayole and Kinangop from women who were enquiring about their sons that, Provincial administration police lorries were used to ferry and gather Kikuyu youths for oath taking recruitment exercise that was performed near a forest in Naivasha, a person who was known to me took that oath and was previously not a Mungiki, he came to understand what he took was the same as Mungiki oath after an exposure through an audio visual documentary I had released exposing Mungiki oath activities.

Were these people in these police lorries Mungiki or selected Kikuyu administration police "who were they"? "Mungiki as an organization had not mobilized its Members to flash out kikuyu youths from their homes for this activity, but they could have used that opportunity to do so. But with police lorries? -this point to a well-coordinated concealed maneuvers".

Administration Police command may not have necessarily given out guns to individual Mungiki Members. Arming civilians would have been a far-fetched idea but selected individual Mungiki leaders may have received these weapons, who would later be traced and eliminated after retrieval.

Nearly all Mungiki leaders who are alleged to have met in an office belonging to Hon Michuki wife all went missing., except Charles Ndungu Wagacha, Naftali Irungu who were killed along Naivasha road and Ndura Waruinge whose heart and soul before God knows what he knows about the retaliatory attacks as alleged by his former comrades.

There is no way uniforms and guns could have been distributed to Mungiki and new Kikuyu youths recruited with the use of administration police lorries without an existing command structure on how to retaliate or defend the community, Mungiki command structure was not directly supporting the government initiative, they were divided, it was not in their policy and ideology to fight such a war, probably ignite it more." Temporary command structure had been formed to execute these plans".

"Another person who was sent to mobilize Mungiki in a Mungiki stronghold was the 'former Juja M. P', Hon George Thuo who convened a meeting and mobilized Mungiki youths from Thika area in a Hotel called Blue Post and after the meeting some youths were transported to Limuru where they converged at Manga Hotel and were joined by other youths from Limuru where they were paid and proceeded to Naivasha".as David states.

Leads from new recruits who were actually given oaths in Naivasha forest and women who inquired about where their sons were taken in Kinangop and kayole supported this fact, that there was a new recruitment exercise that was mobilized and supported by the government. These women pointed fingers to administration police officers in administration police lorries.

Kibaki administration through his Kikuyu trusted lieutenants, John Michuki and Francis kimemia used kwekwe police squad to eliminate all evidence that pointed to their dirty work during 2007/8 post-election violence.

Hon George Saitoti 'former internal security Minister' death has also some elements of cover up, Hon George Thuo 'former M.P Juja' having been a link man to Mungiki leaders in Thika had to shut his Mouth, he couldn't be trusted our cousin', Charles Ndungu Ngugi who was also used at one time by National Intelligent service to contact Mungiki for the Naivasha retaliatory attacks could have been poisoned', he had on these occasions said to be associating with Hon George Saitoti and knew somehow what transpired in Naivasha.

Deputy A.P commandant during the post-election violence period a Mr. Kaunya had to flee, what did he know? nearly all the police officers used for cover up in the elimination of witnesses "the Kwekwe squad" have all faced death to silence them, a cover up by Kibaki administration.

The International criminal court was outwitted, witnesses collected by Waki commission were just pointing issues that had no evidential facts because mobilization of these witnesses was a work that had partisan interests and political influence. These reports which were believed as gospel truth and relied on as evidence by the investigators had errors that needed serious scrutiny before admitted as evidence.

EXTRACTS FROM DAVID WAGACHA RECORDS.

Mungiki was trying everything to see that there was destabilization in the country. Mr. John Maina Kamunya alias "Dr. Maina Njenga" planned on how the message of Mungiki could spread everywhere and get support especially from the Kikuyu diaspora outside Rift valley. He set all these precedence's as prophecies from God. He preached hatred against members of the Kalenjin Communities who he presumed that they would attack and evict all the non-Kalenjin from Rift Valley. He planned and executed the ritual ceremonies throughout the greater cross-section of Kikuyu, Rift Valley, Coast Province, Nyanza Province, Eastern Province and Western Province.

Through his own machinations, pamphlets were scattered in most of the major towns at night in the year 1992 and also it happened again in the areas of Njoro and Elburgon in Nakuru district in 2007. He went on to send some youths in areas of Nakuru district to burn Kalenjin houses at night so that there would be a severe retaliation. This act would have blinded all the Kikuyu people and support Mungiki.

Council of Elders

Due to fear that government led by Kibaki would loose, all the central Kikuyu mafia and Nairobi top Kikuyu businessmen met to lodge the way forward on how the victory would come. Hon. Michuki, PS Kimemia, Kinangop Restaurant Owner Mr. Gathogo and other luminaries started performing Sheep Slaughter gatherings to bless each and every Kikuyu man into elderly and seek a way forward into campaigning for the next government. This issue was extended to young men all who had votes. I myself was called to attend one event in Kiambu region of which I did as I was a great friend to Mr. Gathogo.

Recruitment into Islam

This happened in the year 1998/9 in the Mosque in Eastleigh and spearheaded by the Imam Gathiaka where all the Mungiki leaders 12 nationals were present and given new names. After that the process followed in Jamia Mosque in Capital city for other regional leaders and followers. From Nairobi we went to Matuga college of Islam in Kwale district and other members went to Kikambala in Mombasa. When we discussed at length about the status of our leader John Maina, the Muslim leaders could not trust him in the beginning as a prophet of God and came to a conclusion that he was a "Jinn" just like other angels who might receive messages in the ghost world. In all these events, there was a deal to do export and import businesses together waiting for other missions in Saudi Arabia and other Arab world. We would be exporting food commodities whereas they would be providing us with electronic goods. After The President Daniel Arap Moi discovered the mission, he summoned us in State House Nakuru and totally shunned down this process and warned us to distance ourselves with Islam as it was a dangerous entity to deal with. We co-operated with him but already many members had been recruited fully and strongly to the ranks of Imams. Maina Njenga had become Amir in the movement. To my understanding, the same recruits advanced to Al-Shabaab now.

As I indicated earlier, Maina Kamunya provoked and incited some of the Kalenjin communities into violence that resulted into merciless attacks and evictions of non-Kalenjin tribes in Rift Valley Province. He did this secretly through some of his followers in the backyards in an attempt to seduce all the Kikuyu people to support him and join Mungiki. I recall in 1995 how I accompanied Maina together with another lady from Nairobi and went to Kenyatta's homestead and collected some soil which he performed some rituals to honor the Kenyatta's Kingship in future. He simply mixed the soil with Kenyatta Currency and told us that Kenyatta's powers had started to rule from that time. I can recall how he sent some youth to burn some houses in Likia area of Elburgon and Kihingo area of Njoro in Nakuru district. All this was done in 1992 February and March. He then ran away and sought refuge in Nairobi Mwiki area where his elder father Mr. Muiruri Njoroge lived.

At the same time the pamphlets he planned to be scattered noted that a new President was on the way. "The note read; "KANU REFORMS TO KANC by Dr. Njoroge Mungai"." This issue forced the Kalenjin people to react vigorously as they really thought that they were targeted by Kikuyu people. In 2007 some other leaflets were distributed in Rift Valley and also in Central Kenya and one of the regional leader Mr.

Njoroge Gichere was arrested red handed in Muranga. I remember Maina sending his followers to all districts in Kenya and collect bundles of soil. These bundles were brought to him so that he could perform some rituals that would incite all people everywhere in 2007

CHAPTER SEVEN:

THE 2nd CONSPIRACY; UHURU KENYATTA TO CARRY THE BURDEN.

THE CASE THE PROSECUTOR Vs UHURU KENYATTA.

Mr. Kenyatta was accused to criminally responsible as an indirect co-perpetrator pursuant to article 25[3] a, of the Rome statute for the crimes against of humanity, murder, deportation of forcefully move of population, rape, persecution and other inhuman acts. Case Information Sheet - The Prosecutor v. Uhuru ... - ICC.

The International Criminal Court relied very heavily on a report called Waki Commission, a commission set to investigate the 2007/8 political violence in Kenya, whose work was influenced by political figures and other partisan individuals who were scoring political scores by mobilizing witnesses to appear and record statements to these commission.

A case scenario was the witness from Bunge la mwananchi-People's parliament [....name withheld], who was not a Mungiki member but claimed to be, he had not taken any Mungiki oath and no ordinary Mungiki member would have gone to such high profile meetings, his statement on oath taking was false, his experience was completely something different from the actual Mau Mau or Mungiki oath.

The alleged meetings in Nairobi Club, where he alleged to have met Ambassador Francis Muthaura and Uhuru Kenyatta at Yaya center was his own creation, or he might have heard about them or they never existed, that hearsay required investigation before taken as evidence, he may had had a clue or a lead through hearsay as a friend of Godwin Kamau Wangoe, who both were members of Bunge la mwananchi, a Mungiki representative who went to State house on November 26,2007. His allegations needed investigation not a corroborative statement from another source that turn also to be hearsay.

This was only evidence that linked Uhuru Kenyatta to Mungiki prior to me contacting the International criminal court, as evidence from Waki commission. and Kenya National commission on Human Rights report on a list of shame].

The International Criminal Court had no Mungiki witnesses before I wrote to them, if it had, most probably one witness who and had given some different accounts of events that had not positioned Uhuru Kenyatta as a suspect,

The other fact that the International Criminal Court relied on was the year 2002 general election, Uhuru/Mungiki connection, Mungiki had supported Uhuru Kenyatta presidential ambition, a fact that had no connection with the facts of the case.

My cousin David Waithaka Wagacha was approached by Uhuru lawyers Gillian Higgins and Benjamin Joyes through lawyer Mbuthi Gathenji, 'former Kikuyu M.P' Hon. Guyai and a State House operative a Mr. Charles Waithaka and sought help to establish who were the Mungiki followers that could have been in State House.

Uhuru Kenyatta lawyer Mbuthi Gathenji wanted us to write statements completely refuting that connection and state that Uhuru Kenyatta had no Mungiki connection, they wanted us change the picture painted and not be elaborative on facts.

"We would have arrived on a simple solution but the past tormented us and after a State House operative Charles Waithaka and the then permanent secretary internal security Francis kimemia came into the scene, that changed completely the course of events that followed".

The lawyers were focused in establishing who we could actually recognize from some pictures and list of names of people who had visited state house on 26th November 2007 and they wanted we identify who we knew in the pictures and in the list they had collected from State House Nairobi, probably the "reason of the presence of the State house operative Charles Waithaka", [a name very close to our family names].

The name of the Mungiki representatives who visited state house in this Particular day of Nov 26th, were in the list given. But their serious inquires fell on Bunge la mwananchi witness name [withheld...], whose name was not in the list, we were unable to correctly place him as a Mungiki leader.

After our statements were collected and of course categorically stating to the facts as wanted delivered without elaboration, Uhuru lawyers sought to know if we can be of help by contacting Mungiki leaders in specific locations where they wanted to visit and interview those leaders. Maina Njenga had refused that invitation," waiting for the right opportunity to make a kill", Maina Njenga always aimed on money in most of his dealings. In these interviews we had been perfectly told that there is no monetary compensation except for transport, food and reasonable expenses, phone calls and such.

We were asked to alert Mungiki Leaders in Naivasha where the retaliatory attacks happened, Thika where the initial preparation meeting of the attacks took place, Nairobi Kawangware, kibera areas, and in Nakuru and Eldoret, where Mungiki was said to have done those revenge attacks.

Mbuthi Gathenji and Charles Waithaka had clearly alerted us on the purpose of these statements and we had understood them very well, they are not a fact finding mission but an exoneration exercise and we had therefore alerted these Mungiki leaders not to drag Uhuru in this mad but exonerate him." Mungiki followers would tell a story as is wanted, a lie or truth to them are the same, they are next to one another and to some extend are twins". They would normally ask "what do you want me to tell them"? shying away from any truth. Most of their doings are evil and decoyed.

We took Uhuru lawyers to Thika and Naivasha where they had a chance to interview Mungiki leaders.

"Probably these lawyers realized that, they not getting detailed account of events as were, or the stories looked similar," by then Uhuru initial appearance date with the court was quickly approaching, they instead sought to meet with Geoffrey Machira who took Mungiki to state house on November

26th-2007. A move that "stirred and created repelling forces", between Uhuru Kenyatta lawyers and state house operatives, Francis Kimemia and Ambassador Muthaura.

That interview was set aside and was agreed it was not necessary, the most crucial meeting had burnt some people fingers and was discarded at eleventh hour, Geoffrey Machira and Francis kimemia arranged, "we issue a press statement as Mungiki leaders exonerating Uhuru Kenyatta blaming Maina Njenga and Hon Raila Odinga for witness coaching, we obliged and issued that statement as was required".

 We tried to partner with them but everything looked suspicious, we feared for our lives having known what had transpired earlier and after serious considerations when a Mungiki member was sent to us by the former Gatundu North M.P Patrick Muiruri and Uhuru Kenyatta cousin Ngengi Muigai to talk to us and arrange for a meeting with them, we explored other options

We met with Hon Patrick Muiruri and Hon Ngengi Muigai on two occasions, and in one occasion, Ngengi Muigai told us he represented the family and had been sent to talk to us and came up with a solution on how best, "we can identify the witnesses who had pinned Uhuru Kenyatta on this case", we didn't know how to go about or who were the witnesses, they gave us suggestion on an occasion where Hon John Michuki blasted some of them in state house after they were denied money. They told us," they knew we are able to trace them wherever they are and relied on us for help".

The unfolding events were overwhelming scaring and we had asked Uhuru Kenyatta lawyers for protection from Mungiki leaders. We alerted them on the unfolding events, the plans to trace witnesses and Kimemia induced press statement,

The lawyers asked us to write a letter requesting for that protection but as days passed without assurance of protection and after flashing back the deaths of David brothers, Charles Ndungu Wagacha, George Njoroge Wagacha, and other Mungiki leaders who had in contacts with authorities, our fear overcoming us, we aggressively sought to get audience with Uhuru Kenyatta himself, wishing that probably a word with him would soften our worries, all avenues were hindered and we never saw him.

Francis Kimemia and Geoffrey Machira were in a mission unknown to us.

I evaluated all options and decided to write to the International Criminal Court reporting facts in the ground as they were, and after a very brief period they answered me and arranged ways of communication that would be secure for us.

The international criminal court called me and requested me to meet them with my cousins David Wagacha and Joe Waiganjo in Dar es salaam Tanzania. We had sealed a deal our protection was assured if we can outwit Kimemia and make it to Dar es Salaam.

Our security and protection was guaranteed once we arrive in Dar es Salaam. We left Joe Waiganjo who delayed and by God grace we made it to Tanzania but we realized in our first interview their focus was not how much we knew about what transpired during the 2007/8 general Election but corroborative statement that points to Uhuru Kenyatta and Francis Muthaura to the violence as their summons suggested.

The first interview with us was directed on one single fact did Uhuru Kenyatta contact Mungiki, or met Mungiki or any one of us and did he give any finance for logistics support or any other support during the post-election violence period? they had clearly told us earlier through a phone conversation while in Nairobi that, our protection and security would so much depend on that interview.

We knew going back to Nairobi means death, Ngengi Muigai comments and a public statement financed by Francis Kimemia aired by media houses exonerating Uhuru Kenyatta was as signal to us that the government was committed to fight a war to loose the ties that seemed to expose their dirty works in 2007/8 post-election violence and we were not ready to cooperate with Francis Kimemia.

We wanted protection and post-election violence suspects to face the judges, we wanted Justice for the tribal clashes victims in Kenya and to us it didn't matter which tribe the victims belonged, the evil in the government, to us was unbearable. We thought the International Criminal court would start an investigation on witnesses tampering, as we had been requested to help the Uhuru team, but it seemed they had a different approach.

We had shown Kimemia we would cooperate in full buying time and pondering what to do, David had promised him he would assist him getting an inventory of guns and uniforms that Mungiki members possessed, given by the government or from any other source.

David had tried to alert those that he thought could be having some uniforms and guns and a Mungiki member had volunteered to trace them but knowing Mungiki very well this was a fruitless exercise and it was a game plan, a message to Kimemia," the path continues, the guns and the uniforms were for sale now and retrieving them would cost you a fortune".

"He had earlier sent some police officers to track us and 'our days were numbered, our life hanged on the balance', though he knew we had been interviewed by Uhuru lawyers and therefore he didn't know actually what other programs his other comrades the State house operative a Mr. Charles Waithaka or Uhuru lawyers were up to, God was in our side we outwitted Kimemia and before he could either eliminate David Wagacha whom he had sent to State house Nakuru to collect guns and uniforms," as David alleges. Our way of escape was complete.

Defensive mechanism for survival is natural, unconscious reflex action that sometimes truth or a lie is not what that counts, a human being under duress, trauma, physically and psychologically abused can accept any form of persuasion that can temporarily relieve the insane mental torture that one maybe undergoing, we were no exceptional.

We told the Investigators of the International criminal court exactly all what we knew and what they wanted to hear, to satisfy their conclusions, targets of already drawn lines.

 Facts as we knew them were not important at this stage, a process that we slowly realized after several interviews that took days. We fully analyzed facts as we knew them during the progressive interviews hoping that they will commence an investigation to the leads we gave. We clearly alerted them on false evidence that Mungiki Members can give, especially on such forums where all that is required is a statement.

Mungiki oaths or Mau Mau oaths binds the victims to secrecy and due to fear of consequences, engaging a Mungiki to establish a fact is a fruitless exercise unless the witness undergoes a counselling session, they were on a mission that would not yield anything, we asked them to follow specific leads from new recruits who were specifically recruited for post-election retaliatory attacks in Naivasha, they were adamant and considered that Waki commission had all they required, a wrong concept they had to face it hard challenging their professionalism.

They had erred and out of focus for in all honesty we had no concrete evidence to point on Uhuru kenyatta and their basis of their conclusion from Bunge la mwananchi witness statement was already in the trash can, he had recanted that evidence that had been used to summon Uhuru Kenyatta.

Our reference to" December 30 th 2007" meeting where Uhuru kenyatta was alleged to have dished out money was all hearsay; in fact, we had tried to place that date "December 30 th" as a probable day. We corrected the facts and informed the International Criminal court as necessary

CHAPTER EIGHT:

"Could Mungiki had ignited the tribal clashes?".

PERSONAL OBSERVATION.

Having interacted with Mungiki and understood their mode of operation some allegation on the events that surrounded the post-election violence could have been exaggerated, statements by Mungiki Members or allegations needed an investigative process, just like any other accusation where investigators scrutinize facts and proves them.

One thing that stands out as very mysterious is a fact that the Kalenjin, Kikuyus, and some tribes of Kenya could have fallen into a trap, a seed sowed by the devil, through a prince demon that rules tribes and through manipulation and rituals, the demon stirred their ancestral spirits and awakened them demanding ethnic-Kingdoms, a trace that has a very high percent of truth, Maina Njenga is the main perpetrator of political violence since 1992, 'a Mungiki prophecy,' speaks of a federal government and in that line the demon was leading the populace towards that political arrangement.

Mungiki are masters of propaganda, deceit and lies and through lies and slander," they can paint anything to a color desired", it was the duty and it remain the duty of any investigative authority to establish facts for any meaningful prosecution process.

To Mungiki, it doesn't matter sworn or unsworn statement, signed or unsigned, so long an event is a 'stepping stone' that can be used and discarded, they can engage in anything. Mungiki as an organization could only have fueled the clashes more not necessarily to defend their community, any role they could had played was to ignite more, by God mercies, it didn't go far, their command structure was very divided with some supporting ODM and some PNU. Mungiki was progressing its own mission, its own agenda, establishing an Ethnic-Kingdom that Maina Njenga is the Caliph and that has been its goal riding on government cooperation and support where necessary, Kikuyu politicians had always tried to make a coup to be the caliph and commander of the Mungiki militia but they had been unable, Democratic party tried, Hon David Murathe, Uhuru Kenyatta, Kibaki administration through appointed lieutenants. They all failed, the only option that was left for Kibaki lieutenants was to do a new recruitment for retaliatory attacks in Naivasha.

The leaders that are alleged to have meet government officials in Hon Michuki wife office in Cargen House and especially Ndura Waruinge could only recruit new recruits, Waruinge had no command of Mungiki, such an occasion or meeting was a money making project for Mungiki their slogan is "ni kaogi" "get the money, pretend you are doing something, mobilize some youths, who are not necessarily Mungiki, lead the attack, incite the youths withdraw and disappear", they call it ni "kaogi", meaning be wise here, that's their mode of operation, they only fight their wars ,protecting their "Kirinyaga Kingdom" where Maina Njenga is the 'caliph'.

My bet is most of these attacks were done by ordinary kikuyu incited by Mungiki. Mungiki were busy giving oath to new recruits and according to their prophesy that war was not theirs but for the" fools" referred as 'Babylonians' who didn't heed the call to became a Mungiki. They believe in an "ethnic kingdom" Kirinyaga Kingdom not Kenya and their King is Maina Njenga.

They believe every tribe should fight for its own sovereignty, its own ethnic Kingdom, just as Mau Mau believed in "ithaka na wiyathi", to them Kenya can only be constituted as a federal government.

The International criminal court would have done some serious investigation even though the Kenyan government would have obstructed their investigations, Waki report was a guideline to understand some facts but not evidence based facts, their unprofessional conduct costed them time, resources and shame. They should have charged the middle level perpetrators who would have led them to the high profile.

A deal with the middle level perpetrators on impunity if they testify, would have helped them establish a solid case but their speed and altitude failed them, their very first step to denying justice the victims of the post violence.

The greatest lesson we should learn or endeavor to understand in all this is beyond the guilty or not guilty verdicts in the public court.

Understanding events that led to these atrocities should be our reflection, the reality of Kenya politics and learning is all that is left after all tragedies, some damage are unrepairable though consoling words and tranquility heals hearts. If we were all to live with pain, we would damage many souls and neither should live with pain, I owe my apology to those aggrieved parties that thought I was out to support a lie, my move saved a life and straightened facts and to

Uhuru kenyatta, you can change this path that Kenyans are travelling, a path of ethnic coalition in ethnic Kingdoms, divides the populace more, unfolding events helps those that seek knowledge and wisdom.

Humans should be keen to learn negative forces that influence them and we need to learn some similarities that influence, through manipulation of human lineal descent, be it through race, color, tribe or religion.

First of all, seasons and times determines growth of anything, a right environment, right time, the right location and the right people. Without some natural expectation of a seed sowed in the past, a hope, a lie or true, any new ideology cannot have a foundation on any human being. Nothing is so new in the world, world development, evil or good relays so much on other intelligent forces that influences humans.

Depending on human mind development, good or evil is a moral free will. Humans finds themselves imprisoned in realms of influence that sometimes a lie is construed to be truth and is believed and lived.

If one can openly understand with a mind to learn, the seed behind the origin of Mungiki, and the age of Maina Njenga at that time, his education by then, history of the Kikuyu tribe, believes and culture, then the nature of the Kind of the Prince demon" Jinn" that ruled his being can be drawn and no wonder it is exactly the same as the Prince demon that has awakened the ISIS demanding Islamic Caliphate.

I had drawn some similarities tracing a seed through what been witnessed and believed, testified by reformed Mungiki followers, each step of Mungiki growth, their lineage to a prophecy likened to Koran and Islamic Ideologies that is believed to be the basis of Islamic Caliphate.

Mungiki traced their prophesy to Mugo Kibiru the Kikuyu seer who lived in 18th century, according to the prophecy, after the Kikuyu take the mantle of political leadership from a small tribe which was later seen to be the Kalenjin, that mantle of leadership was to remain with "nyumba ya Mumbi" house Mumbi or among the kikuyus "forever".

Mungiki and Maina Njenga saw interpretation of this prophecy fulfilled through them not any other Kikuyu and according to them it was meant to be a monarchy kind of government with a spiritual leader and Maina therefore considered himself to be the Caliph-King of a Kingdom he referred as "Kirinyaga Kingdom". Messages of prophetic nature from a god called "ngai, [Kikuyu call God the Almighty Ngai but he has a teaching different from the Bible and he got his prophets and priests.] this is a coded god – "ngai" or wa kirinyaga who led them, and on daily message they waited for "ndumeriri" or message from him.

His father Stephen Kamunya Njoroge was also considered inspired with those "ndumeriri 'and he would write these "ndumeriri"-messages in a book that was kept sacred and Mungiki members would visit Maina Njenga or his father seeking divine intervention, blessings of any nature or get new "ndumeriri" to take to their "Matura" villages.

Today, some Kikuyus still wait for the prophetic "kirinyaga Kingdom", some believe it was fulfilled through Mwai Kibaki and subsequently Uhuru kenyatta taking the mantle of leadership in continuation of Kikuyu tribe political leadership. Time will tell if Kikuyus will vote for their political coalition partners the Kalenjin come 2023 an arrangement that gave birth to Jubilee. alliance party.

Every knee will bow and very mouth confess to Him the Word of God Lord Jesus Christ who searches the reins of the hearts and exposes, the deep secrets of men's heart.

Grace calls out with love and faith opens the doors of repentance, which gives birth to harmony, a new dawn.

BY

Joseph   Ndungu:

Glory to God in the highest and
peace to all men.

"COULD MUNGIKI HAD IGNITED THE TRIBAL CLASHES?".

Mungiki scuds.

Mungiki was trying everything to see that there was destabilization in the country. Mr. John Maina Kamunya alias "Dr. Maina Njenga" planned on how the message of Mungiki could spread everywhere and get support especially from the Kikuyu wider community in Central province, He set all these precedence's as prophecies from God. He preached hatred against members of the Kalenjin Communities who he presumed that they would attack and evict all the non-Kalenjin from Rift Valley. He planned and executed the ritual ceremonies throughout the greater cross-section of Kikuyu, Rift Valley, Coast Province, Nyanza Province, Eastern Province and Western Province.

Through his own machinations, pamphlets were scattered in most of the major towns at night in the year 1992 and also it happened again in the areas of Njoro and Elburgon in Nakuru district in 2007. He went on to send some youths in areas of Nakuru district to burn Kalenjin houses at night so that there would be a severe retaliation. This act would have blinded all the Kikuyu people and support Mungiki, a game plan he started from 1992.

A new day breaks forth, free yourself from ethnic-kingdom and be alert, truth sets you free.

GOD BLESS'

THE END.

TRUE STORY

'COULD MUNGIKI HAD IGNITED THE TRIBAL CLASHES'?

TRACING THE EVIL SEED.

JOSEPH   NDUNGU

www.ingramcontent.com/pod-product-compliance
Lightning Source LLC
Chambersburg PA
CBHW051746250726
48659CB00001B/267